KINGDOM MENU

If it's on the menu, then the chef can make it!

SALOME CHIFAMBA

Published by Salome Chifamba

Copyright © 2018. All rights reserved. No portion of this publication may be used, reproduced or transmitted by any means, digital, electronic, mechanical, photocopy or recording without written permission of the publisher, except in the case of brief quotations within critical articles or reviews.

ISBN: 978-0-6483432-0-2 (paperback)

For book orders and enquiries, contact:

Salome Chifamba

Email: schifamb@yahoo.com.au

DEDICATION

To my husband Fidelis and my three cherubs Kudzai, Rumbidzai and Rutendo. The Lord has set a table before us, let us order and 'dig in.'

Many thanks to my husband Fidelis and my daughter Rutendo for all the support with the editing of the book.

My gratitude to my kids for all the prayers.

I thank God for our parents for the wonderful work they all did in raising us up. We would not be where we are today, if it was not for our parents who prayed and spoke words of faith and hope into our lives.

My gratitude to the man of God, Michael Hood for all the work in his ministry, Blood of the Lamb Christian Community and how that has moulded my husband and I to be who we are today.

Many thanks to the man of God Ezekiel Guti and his wife Eunor of Forward in Faith Ministries, whose ministry trained Pastor, Harrison Hungwe and his wife Esther, who led me to Christ and prayed for my deliverance back in 1992. My gratitude to Tadius and Tendai Mawoko, who prayed with us and introduced us to pastor Hungwe and his wife who prayed for my deliverance. I am forever grateful to them for helping me in my journey to be where I am today.

Contents

Preface vii

Introduction ix

1. Is salvation on the menu? Let us place our order shall we? 1

2. Hints and tips on how to pray for our families to be saved 23

3. Scroll down the menu to deliverance 35

4. Healing is on the menu; therefore it is in the kitchen 45

5. No second thoughts about this one – ask for the Holy Spirit 53

6. Provision is on the menu so let us place our order 65

7. Order guidance; it is there on the menu 79

8. Time to grow up 91

9. Expectations of the Kingdom citizens 95

10. Entitlements of restaurant patrons 103

Conclusion: Go tell a friend 109

PREFACE

For many years my husband and I have wanted to share our life journey but we put the idea on hold for a very long time until 2008 when we decided to give it a go. We knew what we wanted to write about but had no idea what to give as a title to the book. I thought of Psalms 23 v 5 where David said 'you set a table before me in the presence of my enemies,' and I thought to use that verse as a connection to the title of my book and to set the whole book in a restaurant. The verse makes me think of a set up in a restaurant where if you are handed a menu in a restaurant, then you know for sure the kitchen staff can make it.

I love praising God all the time and thanking Him for all the things He has done in my life. I have often said this to friends; I like to thank God for what He did for the children of Israel when they left Egypt into the promised land. It was one miracle after another and I like the Red Sea drama more than anything but my life has had its own Red Sea dramas too. In the end, while of course I see what God did for the children of Israel and praise Him for that, I think of my own Red sea situations. So I praise my God for what he has done in my life personally. I want to relate to what the Samaritans said to that woman Jesus met at the well, 'we now believe not for what we have heard but for what we have seen for ourselves'. So I give glory and honour to my God for what He has done in my life.

Introduction

Have you ever noticed that if something is advertised for free, the first question that comes to your mind is what is wrong with it? Car for free! The next thing I expect after that is 'needs some work.' Then I go 'no wonder it's free'. Free food! That's unheard of. Who gives out free food these days? My question always with free things is "what's the catch?" We live in a society where nothing is free for no reason and l am very skeptical of free stuff! Let me take you on a journey. Go ahead and feed your imagination.

So here you are, in a big city, and you are so hungry that you could eat almost anything. You see a sign that says **Kingdom Restaurant** and you decide to go in there to eat.

As soon as you walk in, a very cheerful waitress greets you and asks what you would want to order. You ask for a drink first then the menu. You get a nice cold drink and then you start browsing through the menu to look for something to eat. There you go! Your favourite meal is there so you decide to order it.

Mm hang on a minute, something is not right here. There are no prices on the list on the menu so you wave at the same waitress, who comes straight away to help. 'What would you want to order?' She asks with the same cheerful smile. You point at your favourite meal but you ask how much it costs. The waitress smiles again and assures you that you can order your meal and not worry about payment. That's quite strange. So you thank the waitress cheerfully for her sense of humour and you say to her, 'Thanks for the joke, I really needed cheering up today. So on a more serious note how much is the meal?' Again the waitress smiles back and says politely, 'food here is free. Go ahead and order your meal. You don't have to worry about payment. The owner of the restaurant made a deal with his son a long time ago. The son paid for all the meals and whatever is on the menu is free for all.'

Your reasoning mind warns you to talk to someone else because seriously you are starting to doubt the sanity of the waitress.

You politely thank the waitress and you ask to talk to the manager who comes in a few minutes later to answer your questions. You start to talk to the manager, 'Sorry Sir to bother you on a busy day like this, I wanted to order my meal but then I noticed on the menu there are no prices, so I asked one of your waitresses to explain. Please don't get me wrong she wasn't rude to me at all, she told me that all the meals here are for free and I just thought I should check with management. Nothing against the waitress but free meals seriously!! What restaurant would do business like that?'

The manager clears his throat and starts to smile 'She is right.' The manager explains. Your eyes feel like they are going to pop out of their sockets. 'Sorry what did you say sir?' The manager continues to explain 'I know this sounds strange to all our customers when they first come here but it is true. All meals here are free. The owner's son signed a deal with his father a long time ago. He paid for all the meals so that whoever comes here enjoys whatever they want.'

Logic tells you to stand up and leave. Something here doesn't make sense. Who wants to run a business for no profit especially if they have staff wages to pay? You look around and you see people come in and go and eating and laughing and you decide to ask more questions.' How much did the son pay to cover for all these meals?' 'He paid with his life.

Yes he died that you and I can come to this restaurant, sit down and order whatever is on the menu for free.'

That's it! You don't want to know more! What father would sacrifice his son for other people? Who would in their right mind sign such a deal with their son for the world? You think this is maybe a practical joke so you check the date. It is not April fool's day, this is August. Ok the best way is to ask other customers, that way you know what is going on. So you thank the manager and excuse yourself to go and talk to a couple sitting next to your table that seem to be having a good time, looking very relaxed. They look very descent so they would not lie, you think quietly. 'Excuse me and sorry to interrupt, I just wanted to check something with you guys. Is it true that all the meals are free here because of a deal between the owner and his son?' The couple smile at you and nod their heads, 'Yes it is true that's why we come here everyday, we practically live here.'

Ok, people here do sound weird, so you decide to leave but then the nice couple stop you, 'why don't you give this a try? Order a meal and see if they charge you. We are telling the truth. This is the most amazing place in the whole world.'

'Yeah right!' You say that inwardly.

Could this be real? The menu list is very long and surely they must be able to provide what is on the menu, but for free? Well that does not sound real or normal but you sit down to give it a try. You notice there are over three thousand things on the list of the menu. Nothing makes sense so you sit down to ponder on the words of the manager and the waitress.

Then something clicks in your head. The only verse in the bible that even non-Christians know flashes in your mind, 'For God so loved the world that He gave His only begotten Son that whosoever believes in Him should not perish but have eternal life.' There you go! You remember that verse from Sunday school. God loved you and me that if we believe in His son we are free to enter into His kingdom so that if we are handed the menu for the kingdom we can go ahead and order what we want and be assured that we will get it. Being a citizen of the kingdom is not a right but a privilege. You and I did not deserve to be called children of God but once we become children of God by believing in His Son Jesus, then we have rights as citizens of the kingdom of God, to everything that belongs to the King. Above all, we have eternal life which is number one on the menu for free. What a deal! What a deal!

You start to giggle in your heart. You start to realise that this is not a practical joke, it is for real. You relax, sit down at your table, pick up the menu and smile. What a deal, what a deal! This is going to be so much fun. You look at the menu to pick what you want to order knowing it will be free and available.

MENU

Main Meals

Manager's Special: Salvation

Served with lots of sacrificial love on a bed of Grace. This is served to you and the rest of the family. It is to whosoever is willing.

Ephesians 2 v 8-9

You eat this meal by believing in your heart and confessing with your mouth that Jesus is Lord.

Price: Free

The Holy Spirit

You can order this meal as soon as you receive your salvation meal. He is served with love, joy, peace, faithfulness, kindness and longsuffering.

Price: Free

Deliverance

From the Chef himself. He who calls upon his name shall be saved. The Chef with lots of love made a public spectacle of the enemy. The enemy has no power over you. Chef Jesus, is the one who calls you out of darkness into His marvelous light.

Price: Free

Financial Breakthrough

Mathew 6 v 33

To get this meal it starts with you being a giver then it will be given back to you.

Malachi 3 v 10

It is through our giving that financial breakthroughs come. This is always available in the kitchen.

Price: Free

Forgiveness

Served immediately after the offence, all you have to do is confess your sins to the Lord.

1 John1 v 110

You can share this with some of the diners in the kingdom just in case they offend you too.

Ephesians 4 v 31-32, Mathew 6 v 14-15

Price: Free

Healing

The Manager took all our sicknesses and diseases and healed us all. It was all done on the cross.

Isaiah 53 v 4-5

Price: Free

Restoration

Joel 2 v 25

Restoration is for everything and everyone. The thief comes to kill, steal and to destroy but Jesus came that you might have life and life to the full. With all confidence you can order this for everything that the enemy took away from you. You will have it back and with proceeds (profits). It will backfire on the enemy.

Price: Free

<u>Children</u>

Joel 2 v 25

They come in all different forms, shapes and sizes. They are all tailor made to suit all parents. Can be challenging too but they are a great delight to have.

I Sam 1 V 1-20

Price: Free

Beverages

Do not be drunk with wine but be filled with the Holy Spirit and get drunk for real!!!! When the day of Pentecost had fully come they were filled with the new wine. They then went on to turn the world upside down.

Living water

Price: Free

Desserts

Love

Joy

Peace

Faith

Miracles

Word of Knowledge

Word of wisdom

Prophecy

Tongues

Price: Free

CHAPTER 1

IS SALVATION ON THE MENU? LET US PLACE OUR ORDER SHALL WE?

A true fact about all restaurants is that if something is on the menu then it is in the kitchen. So as you sit down to place your order you see a meal called Salvation, top on the list and you decide to order it. Salvation is when a person has a personal encounter with the Creator of the Universe our God, by His Grace. John 1 v12 says 'But as many as received Him, to them He gave the right to become children of God, to those who believe in His name.' Friend, if you believe in Jesus Christ as your Lord and Saviour, confess with your mouth that He is Lord, then you are saved.

It is like falling pregnant, (girls back me up on this). What happens is the little person inside of you starts to run your life. This is for real, one month or two after conception, depending on individuals, you start the morning sickness. That is not pleasant but that is a sure sign something has happened. All of a sudden you, who never liked yoghurt, become a big fan of it. You just cannot rest until you taste the yoghurt and whose fault is it? The person growing inside of you. A woman's diet changes drastically with pregnancy and the physical looks too. Dressing changes and she can be off some things too.

The same applies to a born again Christian. For no reason, the cravings for drugs or alcohol that used to control you are gone. No one can explain that very well but as soon as you open the door for Jesus in your heart, He starts to run your life for your good. The desire to gossip is all gone and before you know it, you just want to read the bible, the word of God. You get all excited you want to tell all your friends (and this can be very tricky. Your friends might start doubting your sanity but it does not matter). You think twice before you join in to gossip about the boss at work.

Jesus Himself summed it all up perfectly in John 3 v8 "the wind blows where it wishes, and you hear the sound of it, but cannot tell where it comes from and where it goes. So is everyone who is born of the Spirit." You surely cannot see the wind but you see its effects. You cannot really say there is salvation over there in that church but you can surely see its effects on individuals. Paul explains this in his second letter to the Corinthians 5 v 17-18 "Therefore, if anyone is in Christ, he is a new creation; old things have passed away; behold all things have become new. Now all things are of God who has reconciled us to Himself through Jesus Christ, and has given us the ministry of reconciliation."

Salvation makes one brand new. You feel refreshed beyond human understanding.

You start thinking in a new way and seeing things and people differently.

This is not instant but as we grow in Christ, we begin to see things in a different way. Love that we never felt before just comes naturally. You who never loved Gospel music will start enjoying it. Listen dear friend, being born again does not make you a boring person. It does not mean you cannot be fashionable in your dressing or you cannot go to a party. Here is the good news. You will not be asked to shave your head the minute you walk into a church nor will you be asked to throw away all your fashionable clothes and be given the gowns that Moses wore in his time! God is not interested in what you wear friend, but he is keen on the inside person (of course you have to dress properly you cannot rock up at church or anywhere in your birthday suit!). Young people feel this way sometimes, they think church is only for older people who have got nothing else to do on a Sunday morning. Being in a relationship with God is so much fun. It can't even be compared to any 21st birthday parties you have been to!

Jesus put it this way in Mathew 13v 44, "Again, the kingdom of heaven is like treasure hidden in a field, which a man found and hid; and for joy over it he goes and sells all that he has and buys that field.'

Mathew 13 v45-46, "Again, the kingdom of heaven is like a merchant seeking beautiful pearls, [46] who, when he had found one pearl of great price, went and sold all that he had and bought it'

In the two parables, the message I am getting is the value placed on the Kingdom and being part of it. It is likened to very important things in our lives, like treasure and pearls. The people in the parables went and sold everything that they had to get the kingdom.

I always imagine a man going home to his wife announcing that they were going to sell everything they have like a house and cars just to get the kingdom. Surely most of us women, if our husbands came home saying that, would ask the only logical question, 'what's in it for us?" The answer should be the same. 'Everything is in the kingdom". This is the truth about the kingdom of God. Everything we want or need, every question we have, every answer to prayer we need is in the kingdom of God. Being a citizen of the kingdom of God is the highest calling any human being can ever have. Seeking that kingdom and the relationship with the king should be the priority of every soul on earth.

In the two parables, Jesus mentioned how the people in the stories gave up everything to gain the kingdom. There is a lot we give up to have a good relationship with the king once we become citizens. We do not exclude ourselves from the world but there are some things in life that we have to let go of as citizens of the Kingdom. Some partying might not be good for us as children of God, so it is ok to say no to some things even if it means we have to disappoint even people we love.

Jesus summed it all up in Mathew 6 v 33, 'But seek first the kingdom of God and His righteousness, and all these things shall be added to you.' All we need to do and focus on is our relationship with our King and everything else that we seek for in life, will be added to us. Let us make seeking God our number one priority. I tell you friend, you will never regret it.

When the kingdom of God has taken over our lives all the other kingdoms that would have been controlling our lives, have to leave. Your life will be under new management and a new government. You will have a new constitution to follow and new principles to run your life. Your language changes to suit the new government in your life.

When the kingdom of Great Britain colonised my country Zimbabwe, things changed. A new language came in called English, from the British and it became the official language of my country. Our lifestyle changed because of the colonial master. We started wearing clothes instead of the traditional skin aprons (nhembe in Shona), because of the British. I do not think skin aprons would have been working for us still! Thank God for the new clothes. We started eating and drinking different drinks and foods from what we used to have, because of the British. The infrastructure of Zimbabwe changed, because of the British. Our education system changed so did the health system. New crops were introduced in agriculture, because of the British. (I am not hung up on what happened back then; I am just trying to illustrate a point). You could tell that a new government had taken over our country.

What I am saying is Britain did not come to accommodate Zimbabwe but to take over and have control. That is what happens when we become citizens of the kingdom of God. The kingdom of God does not accommodate our bad habits and lifestyle; it takes over and controls our lives for our good. We are the ones who will benefit. We even become kings too that is why Jesus is called the King of kings. You and I do not become subjects and get exploited, but we become kings too and joint heirs with the King himself. We are entitled to whatever belongs to the King! Now that is a different type of Colonisation and that I would want in my life.

Our language changes. We will have the language of heaven as our official language. The promises of God become our new language. We will not speak like the world speaks. Here is how the world speaks. 'Nothing ever changes in life, my kids will never change I guess that is my lot in life, my marriage will never make it, my spouse is a loser, it is difficult to have a descent business in this world, etc.' This is how the world speaks and we all maybe used to speak like this until heaven took over.

Now we stand on the word of God. His promises become our new language. 'All things are possible with God, my children are blessed, they are known among the gentiles, people see them and acknowledge them, that they are the posterity whom the Lord has blessed, God makes a way in the wilderness and rivers in the desert.'

'Friend, I could write books and books on the promises of God. These are just a few that I have pulled out to counteract what the world says about life.

God shifts things in our lives and makes us brand new again. Our lifestyle changes as the King brings in a new normal for us.

Now that we have an idea of what happens when one is saved, does anyone want to order that on the menu? It is for free, remember and you do not have to do anything to deserve it. It is by God's grace that we are saved and that means unmerited favour. We all deserved hell but God Himself became man and came down from Heaven to die on the cross for you and me that if we believe in His Son then we become His children. John 1 v 12, "But as many as received Him, to them he gave them power to become children of God, to those who believe in His name".

Feeling guilty that you have messed up too much and you are too dirty to be cleansed by His blood? Well I have good news for you, you are redeemable just check out the genealogy of Jesus in the first chapter of Matthew then you will know that you and I have got a chance.

Rahab commonly known as the 'harlot' is in the bible as one of the great grandmothers of Jesus. If I were God I would not have picked her. I would have picked a pastor's daughter instead but that is not so with our God. He picked her to show us that no one is beyond salvation. The woman ran a brothel but got her family saved when she helped the Jewish spies who had come out to spy out Jericho. Check Joshua chapter 2.

Jacob the liar and trickster is there. He tricked his brother Esau of his birth right. Talk about David the man after God's heart! He did big, took someone else's wife (Bathsheba) and killed the husband (Uriah). Solomon was the product of that relationship between Bathsheba and David, a very shameful union, but Solomon is one of the ancestors of Jesus. By the way, God is not promoting promiscuity here, but he is saying no one is beyond his love and forgiveness. Ruth was a Moabite but she became the great grandmother of Jesus. Her background was not that flash either. Moabites were descendants of Lot when his daughters made him drunk and they slept with their dad after their mother turned into a pillar of salt on their way out of Sodom and Gomorrah. Well that is incest isn't it? That was Ruth's background, she was a descendant of a product of an incestuous relationship. Look, it does not matter how messed up you are. God will take you just as you are and make you a new creature. No one is beyond redemption. 'As far as the east is from the west, so far has He removed our transgressions from us' (Psalm 103v12). There we go my friend, east and west never meet so that is how far God has removed our sins from our records.

I like the fact that the Bible does not white wash its characters by presenting them as holy as angels to us. If I look at some of the characters God used, then I have hope that He will use me too. Look at Saul before he was Paul! Who would have trusted such a persecutor of the church to preach the good news? Well God did. Someone said if there is a person who is good at gambling, it's God Himself. He has trusted you and me to spread the good news that He loves us all but sometimes don't we miss it all and spread something else!

God has got a sense of humour I must say, He even saved me! Born in a somewhat Catholic family (we later moved to be Methodist then back to being Catholics) I had not so much as heard anything like salvation. We went to church when we were little and when I grew up, I went to church to get out of the confines of a boarding house where I did all my high school education. Then later on, I went to church so I could prepare myself for when I had to get married in church, which I did to my high school sweetheart.

My family and I believed in ancestral worship which is very common among the Shona people of Zimbabwe. What happens is, the Shona believe there is God (Mwari) but they pray to God through the dead or ancestors. When Christianity was brought to Zimbabwe and the bible clearly pointed out that the only way to the Father is through His Son Jesus Christ, we the Shona thought that this was another attempt by the colonisers to take over our culture. So many resisted the message of the bible and I do not blame anyone for this because its only by GRACE that we believe in Jesus, otherwise no one works out his own salvation.

I never pretended to be a Christian, I went to church for different reasons. I used to think that people who were Christian were abandoning their culture and were westernised. If anyone tried to tell me about Jesus, I would always defend my traditional beliefs and boy wasn't I rude to Christians!

At the age of ten I had this life changing experience happen to me. This is what they call in my language 'kusvikirwa". I was possessed by a spirit of a dead person. In the bible this is called demon possession but in my culture I became a spirit medium. This I thought was a good thing for me because I thought that would boost my self-esteem since I thought that would make me someone very important in the family. Wasn't I wrong?

I started to have dreams that would scare me all the time. I would get sick just by getting into a car or bus. I could not put perfume on or make up on because the smell of perfume would make me sick. One day I trimmed my eyebrows and my whole face became swollen! All my friends at school commented that I looked older than my age. I was teased at school for looking old. My self-esteem went to ground zero when one day at the age of 18, I walked into church (wanted to impress the boyfriend, who I married later on). This lady who looked like she was in her 50's stood up for me and said in my language 'amai tokupai pekugara here' which means madam, can I offer you a seat. In my culture you only offer a seat to someone who is older than you or a pregnant woman. So for this woman to offer me a seat while all the other youth were being told to go and sit at the back in the hall, made me feel really hurt. I wanted to cry. I could not believe that this woman thought I was older than her! I must have looked 65 or older to her. Now that really made me start to worry about my life. I told the lady who had offered me a seat that I was a youth and she looked like she was going to pass out. She did not hide it in her response to me really. She said very slowly 'Oh you are a youth really my child, then go and sit at the back with the others'. Her tone of voice made me realise she was not convinced at all that I was only a young girl. That killed my self-esteem and I felt gutted.

When I finished equivalent of year 10 (form 4 in Zimbabwe), I went to live in the big city Harare to finish my high school. My brother and his wife had bought a house in a suburb called Unit J Chitungwiza, so I went to live with them for a few weeks while I waited for a place in boarding school, at the new high school I was going to attend. Next door to my brother's house was the Chifamba family. Now there were three boys there and I really liked the middle one. Well I think he did too so he asked me out and I said yes. So Fidelis and I started dating when I was in high school until I finished university then we got married.

One thing that worried me about this boyfriend of mine was what he talked about every time he saw me. He talked about Jesus all the time to the point I was starting to get worried that he was not ok somehow. So I summoned my friends at university and told them about my boyfriend and how he talked about Jesus all the time. Boy didn't they laugh at him! We thought he was lost and needed help. One of my friends even commented that Fidelis talked about Jesus as though he was family and we laughed. Seriously what boyfriend talks about Jesus all the time to his girlfriend? I wanted to go to the movies to watch 'Pretty Woman" or 'Dirty Dancing". I did not know I was sitting on a gold mine. I made it clear to him that I was not Christian and I did not plan on becoming one and my family was to be left out of this whole plan. I do not even know why he still believed I could be wife material anyway, but he did and married me in 1991.

So when I got married I thought I could carry on having the best of both worlds. I could still have church and my African traditional religion. I was ready to blend in with the flow since my husband's family all went to church. I thought being a Christian meant going to church on Sunday with the family then back to 'normal life' after, which I did, but that is not how it should be I must confess.

I was baptised and confirmed but had no idea I could have a personal relationship with God. Let us put it this way, I had no reason to think like that. I thought I had it all. I had married my high school sweetheart, I had a job, I had a baby, my husband had a good job, we had a company flat and car. Wow! I thought I had it all. The last thing on my mind then was being serious with God. I used to wonder why some people took this thing called Christianity too far. Church on Sunday for an hour was ok with me then life back to 'normal' for the rest of the week.

When we got married I brought to my husband a bag full of African herbs (certainly not spices). These I believed were going to look after us and our kids. I was not even ashamed of them because I did not see anything wrong with them. So I showed them to my husband and believe me, the look on his face was disturbing to me. He looked like I had just shown him a live snake in my bag. He took the herbs and flushed them down the toilet one by one. Now that made me mad at him. How dare he throw away my source of strength and protection! That marked our first fight as husband and wife. Fidelis said to me that God looks after us and does not need help from herbs. For a non-Christian, that was a huge blow but he was right only that I did not know that yet!!!

Then something happened that changed my life completely. I fell sick in 1992. I had no idea what was wrong with me, all I know is within weeks I had lost lots of kilos. I was not a big girl then (never been anyway) so I actually needed to put on and not lose weight. The most worrying thing for us as a young family were the voices I used to hear at night. I could hear death threats and our baby used to scream as if he was seeing scary things. He would cling on to me like a baby does when they are scared. Each time I went to bed, my pillow would feel like it was going down a pit and that scared me a lot. I would hold on to the bed rail screaming for help and I could see my husband was scared and worried. One night we decided to sleep in the car because the house was not liveable any more due to the voices I would hear all the time threatening to kill me. That night, my husband drove around the whole town of Victoria Falls just to give us a break from the mosquitoes and also to help our baby go to sleep. Our marriage was heading for divorce in no time at all. I knew in my heart that my marriage was not going to last. Who wants to live with a wife who is always sick and is hearing voices in the house? Who wants a wife who cannot enjoy a ride in a car? Who wants to sleep in a car every night in front of your house? I would not have blamed Fidelis if he had let me go. There were lots of complications around intimacy too. (Cannot go into details on that one, but that would have ended my marriage if God had not intervened).

All this time my husband had no idea I was possessed by a spirit. I did not think that LITTLE detail of my life was necessary to mention! I was worried that I would lose him so I did not mention that when we were dating. Plus I was naïve enough to think that the spirit had left when I gave back the beads I used to wear. (They were very ugly looking black and white beads that used to have me teased at school a lot by both teachers and other students).

So when all this was happening my husband confronted me one day about my spiritual life. He already knew my background. I never made it a secret to him that I did not believe in God, so that part he knew. He had an idea of what he was getting, but that I was possessed by a spirit, he had no idea. I think he had become suspicious after all that was happening so he confronted me. I had to tell him the truth. Gee I have never seen a man cry like that. I was scared and I thought my marriage was over. I felt like an unfaithful woman who had been caught cheating on her husband. Later on, Fidelis told me that the first thing that came to his mind was he was going to take me to Harare to Father Michael Hood so he could pray for me. We did not know God had other plans. I kept on deteriorating and one day I went to work only to be asked to go back home by a very concerned Principal of the school where I was teaching. I must have really looked shocking.

I went to hospital one day when I thought I could not handle it any more. Before the Doctor could see me, I passed out in the waiting room and the next thing I woke up to an announcement from a very concerned Doctor that my blood pressure was very low. So I was admitted in hospital and the next time they checked my blood pressure, it was very high because the news that my blood pressure was low earlier on, had scared me. So there I was in hospital and the doctors were trying to figure out what was wrong with me. They did blood tests to see if I had malaria which came back negative but the doctors did not want to take any chances so they put me straight on a drug called Fansidar for malaria. I was not getting any better so the doctor put me on Quinine for cerebral malaria but that did not make me feel any better. My ears were blocked from the effects of the drug and that made me worry and my blood pressure kept going up.

One night I woke up on my hospital bed to find all the hospital staff around my bed. That scared me and I became suspicious especially when

I found one of my friends who was a nurse there, holding my hand and praying for me. The whole set up made me think I was dying because I was not that important to need all the staff taking care of me at once. So I asked my friend what was going on and she answered me by asking me what was wrong with me which I could not answer. All I knew was that I was sick and I felt darkness all around me. So they continued to monitor me all night that night and Victoria Falls being a small town, all my friends would have been told that I was not that well so the next day a friend of ours rocked up with his pastor. He introduced me to his pastor and told me that they wanted to pray for me. This was the first time for me to hear of someone wanting to lay hands on me and pray for me. I was not sure if prayer would do me any good but I was so sick so I said yes. The pastor then held my hand and prayed for less than five minutes and left.

Before I could make anything out of this I felt this heaviness lift off my shoulders and I felt new. It is hard to explain the feeling but I could say I felt fresh and renewed and I thought that would not last, but that got me out of hospital after the doctor checked on my progress that morning. All I know is I felt very well. I went home and started what I could call a new life. I asked my husband if we could go and see the pastor and his wife at their house. The pastor then agreed to see us and invited us to his house for further prayer.

I was always skeptical of the Pentecostal churches having been brought up in traditional churches. So I had my reservations until this pastor and his wife from ZAOGA prayed for me. I told them everything about my life (you do not hide things when you need help and your life is hanging on a piece of thread). They asked me first of all to go and fast which I did. I had never heard of that and had never done that before. That evening after fasting all day, I went back to their house and they prayed for me. I cannot explain fully what happened because some parts I seriously do not remember. All I know is, that night, something heavy and black left me. This dark feeling left me and I felt new and light on the shoulders.

They asked me to receive Jesus in my heart which I did. They counselled me on my beliefs and taught me how to pray, fast and read the bible. All my skepticism about Pentecostals were gone in a flash!

I can identify with the psalmist David in Pslams30v1-3.

'I will extol You, O Lord, for You have lifted me up,

And have not let my foes rejoice over me.

² O Lord my God, I cried out to You,

And You healed me.

³ O Lord, You brought my soul up from the grave;

You have kept me alive, that I should not go down to the pit.'

I could have died, lost my marriage and gone to hell for sure but my God saved me. He gave me abundant life. He healed me and healed my marriage. He saved my life from death. I could go on and on.

I am forever grateful to the friends who took me to their pastor and I will always remember the pastors who led me to Christ as well as the founder of that church because they did not judge me for all my unbelief but helped me to be where I am today. I am also grateful to my husband for being there for me and not sending me away to my family. I know that sickness led me to Jesus and I am not saying it is good to be sick but for me, if it was not that I got sick, I would not have thought of giving my life to Christ. Yes it did backfire on the enemy. What the enemy meant for harm, God used it for my good.

After I got delivered I went to visit my in laws and I went to church with them one Sunday morning. After the service, I went outside with my mother in law to say hello to some of her friends. This particular friend of hers came and said hello just like everybody else did but when she saw me she stopped to ask my mother in-law who I was. My mother in-law casually responded to her that I was her second daughter in-law, Fidelis' wife. The friend looked quite confused so she went away then came back to ask again who I was and mum again repeated the same answer. The friend asked again politely 'so is this Fidelis' wife you mean?' and my mother in-law said yes. The friend asked again 'so this is Fidelis' wife, the one that got married in 1991 at St Theresa's Church?' This time my mother in law looked a bit annoyed by her friend's questions so she asked why she was asking all those questions. The friend said clearly 'well she looks very young now I did not recognise her.' Now that got my attention. I looked younger now which means I looked old before! I did not think it was that noticeable after being delivered that God restored my youth. I looked my age for the first time. That made me feel very good I must say. One day I went to work and a friend looked at me so intently and said in my language 'Salome you look so refreshed like someone who has just had a shower,' I cannot explain how I felt about all these new comments.

I cannot say thank you enough to Jesus for setting me free. In fact I could never repay Him for saving me but as long as I live I will tell the world of all that He did for me. Since 1992, I have walked the journey of faith and have stumbled a lot of times but let me encourage someone who thinks they have been too far away from God, that there is hope in God. Yes you can be saved my friend. Jesus actually made a statement one day when He said that He, 'didn't come for the virtuous but for the sinner or the lost."

Well if salvation for the sinner is on the menu, smile at the waitress and order it now because it is in the kitchen. Do not ask the waitress how that will happen just ask and it will be served for you. Trust me the bible says, 'if you confess with your mouth the Lord Jesus and believe in your heart that God has raised Him from the dead, you will be saved." No dramas. You need to come to the Lord just as you are. The price for our salvation has already been paid for. It would be an insult to God to add anything else to the cross. It was finished on the cross. He did it all for us. We do not have to add anything more. Would you want to confess with your mouth and believe in your heart that Jesus is Lord? Would you say this prayer with me?

Lord Jesus I invite you in my heart and I believe you are my Saviour and that you died on the cross for me. Forgive me of my sins and wash me with your blood. Fill me with your Holy Spirit and make me a new person. Amen.

Friend that prayer, short as it is, will do the trick and then we all grow from there. See! You do not have to ask how God changes your heart because no one can explain that. Jesus said that you will not see the wind blow but you will certainly see the effects of it. I will speak for myself, I am still a work in progress and I do not know when I will be finished but Paul said he was not yet there either. Well that is encouraging! If a spiritual giant like Paul confessed he was still trying to get there then you and I can sit back and allow God to do a work in us.

Philippians 3v12-14 says "Not that I have already attained, or am already perfected but I press on, that I may lay hold of that for which Christ Jesus has also laid hold of me. Brethren, I do not count myself to have apprehended; but one thing I do, forgetting those things which are behind and reaching forward to those things which are ahead. I press toward the goal for the prize of the upward call of God in Christ Jesus." See now, the past has to be behind and we have to press on towards eternal life despite how many times we fall. God does not expect us to do it all by ourselves. He helps us to grow by the power of the Holy Spirit.

So as you sit in that restaurant, look at the menu very carefully and if you feel you have never had an experience called salvation, wave your hand at the waiter. Yes, go ahead and order it and you and your household will be saved, and then you can all speak the same language and worship the same God. If you already are a believer in Christ Jesus, you sure can also press an order for your loved ones. And yes don't you worry about the payment; it has all been taken care of by the owner of the restaurant's Son as you have already been told.

One person who challenges me in the Bible is Rahab, commonly known as the harlot. When the men of Israel went out to spy on Jericho,

Rahab helped to hide those men. That was very kind of her but she did not stop there. She went on to sign a deal with the men. The deal was when the men of Israel came to attack Jericho; she asked that she and her family be saved. The men agreed to the deal on condition that Rahab would tie a scarlet cord on her door, that way, the men of Israel would spare her family. Anyone of the family members not in the house with Rahab at the time of the attack would not be the Israelites' responsibility which was fair enough. So the deal was done and to this day there are some descendants of Rahab in Israel. But can you see what Rahab did? She could have just asked for herself to be spared but she remembered her family. Fellow Christian, let us do it for our families too. Let's order salvation for them. Just a word of encouragement to you dear Christian, do not give up on that family member. No one is beyond redemption. There is no such thing as a right off to God. He himself said it in Jeremiah 32v27 'Behold I am the God of all flesh, is there anything that is too hard for me?' The God of all flesh, that is all of us human beings. What that means literally is nothing and no one is too hard for God.

You convinced you can order that now for that son of yours who has been on drugs since he was 16? Maybe it's your spouse; please do not give up praying for them, God answers prayers and this much I can tell you. You do not have to worry how God is going to save your brother who has never set foot in church. You do not have to worry about that. God never runs out of ideas. He can use anything to touch people's lives so just go ahead and order salvation for your family. It is in the kitchen the staff behind the scenes can handle that.

I ordered salvation for my family a long time ago and ever since God has been setting my family free one by one. One of my sisters was having some issues in her life that she could not handle and before I became Christian I used to go everywhere with her looking for help. We went to witch doctors for help but I can assure you nothing changed in her situation. We tried this and that and the so called 'prophets' where my sister would be given these weird concoctions. Why we all thought a mixture of eggs, milk and raspberry cordial would change things is beyond me. If all is not well in one's life, one can look for help in all sorts of places and I do not judge anyone for doing this because if you have never been in someone's else's shoes you cannot understand why they go anywhere for help. Its only when by the grace of God we get saved that we know the truth, that our only source of help is God and God alone.

I tried to talk my sister into praying for her situation after I had been saved but she never listened to me. I happen to be the eighth in a family of nine, so you can understand why no one listens to me. One day my sister rang me and I think that day she had reached the end of the rope. She had had enough and she was ready to give up and she told me that she had found this lawyer who was going to fix her problems and get her out of her misery. She explained to me that this lawyer was very good and was going to make sure she would get a good deal. I tried talking her out of that but again she reminded me how old I was then and how little experience I had about situations like hers. I told her that I knew of a lawyer who is the best in town, and there I think I must have got her attention because she paused on the other end of the phone. 'Who? 'She asked. 'Jesus.' I answered. I knew then that she was going to hang up on me but I told her that I would talk to my lawyer Jesus on her behalf.

Let me encourage you dear friend, do not give up on anyone in your family. My sister months later gave her life to Christ and things turned around in her life and now her family is crazy for Jesus and every day I thank God for her life. All the Glory is to God for answering prayers.

Psalms 65 v 1-2 confirms this,(NKJV).

Praise is awaiting You, O God, in Zion;

And to You the vow shall be performed.

² O You who hear prayer,

To You all flesh will come.'

Did you get that? God hears our prayers.

A friend of mine gave her life to Christ back in 2008 and a couple of weeks after; she told me how she had lost the appetite for alcohol. I wanted to scream with joy but I restrained myself in front of my friend (I did not want to scare my friend out of the kingdom) but I must admit I was thrilled for my friend. She has since been a different person and it is so noticeable.

Just so you know salvation is not just for a few chosen ones, I asked a friend of mine Evi Muldoon to allow me to share her testimony of how God saved her and healed her in 2006. Here is her story and I hope this will encourage you not to give up on yourself or anyone you love.

"Hi I'm Evi, and I want to share with you a little of my faith journey and my personal experience of healing prayer.

On October 8 2006 the first healing prayer service was held in Port Pirie in the church I was attending.

I had been a regular church goer, so I didn't need to go out of my way to attend the service. I'd been invited by a close friend and I went more out of curiosity and to keep my friend happy. To say I was a skeptic was an understatement. I considered myself too practical – scientific even- to believe that anything would happen as a result of people praying over me. If I was wrong – bonus!

So what did I bring for prayer – well nothing much, I thought. After all I was doing quite OK, thanks. I went to church regularly.

There were just one or two things that were a bit of a problem in my life– but God wouldn't be interested in these little things – would he?

I was pretty stressed out, tired, always rushing never enough time for anything but the essentials and usually running late. I found it hard to get going most mornings, and usually had to have a few drinks at night to "unwind". Didn't sleep that well – after all I had a lot on my mind - my work and all that.

Oh and then there was the weight – well that was just middle age, over work and no time or energy to do something about it – probably the junk food too, but I'd get around to fixing that.

I should mention the asthma –which was mostly seasonal but gradually spreading from spring through the rest of the year and needing more time off, more treatment. (At its worst I had to take 25 mg prednisolone, 2 puffers, the nebuliser and occasional antibiotics). The smoking contributed but that was a habit I'd get around to changing.

I wouldn't even mention my blood pressure except that I spent a bit of time in the Emergency Department at work when it was way too high – but that was probably because of the asthma playing up, and the stress. (Actually I was scared to go home one day because I live alone and I was afraid I'd have a stroke or something.)

Oh there was also this skin cancer thingy on my hairline that the hairdresser had been hassling me to get looked at but I hadn't had time.

I also took along the notion that **my** life was **my** problem and **my** business. I had to go at it alone. As a single parent I'd come to believe that I had to rely on my own resources for everything – no one could or would help - not family, not friends. After all you shouldn't owe people, and who could be relied on? What about God? – Well, God is only interested in the big things like peace in the Middle East.

My notion of God was that He was far off, and He loved us as a group in a sort of philosophical way. Salvation came with baptism, and I was baptised. The rest was up to me.

So, as I came to the prayer team that day – I didn't have anything much that God would be interested in.

Then I sat down, and out of my mouth came so many things that

I hadn't even thought about – my Dad and my brother mostly and what they needed.

Suddenly good old logical me was so overwhelmed by emotion. I can't even tell you what emotion, but it involved a lot of tears and sobs. Nobody was more surprised than me!

As the team began to pray I heard someone ask the Lord to "lift these burdens" from me.

I don't have words to describe what happened after that except that, like St Thomas in the upper room, I knew that Jesus is alive, knows me personally, loves me personally, no matter what, and had somehow been waiting for me to ask Him to help. The only prayer I could manage was the shortest one I'd ever said - "My Lord and My God".

That encounter has changed everything and that's no exaggeration.

I have discovered that the promises in God's word are true and apply to me, to you, to anyone who comes to Him.

1 Peter 2: 24 "by His wounds you have been healed."

I don't have asthma at all, any season; I am over 30 kg lighter; my blood pressure is well under control and that skin cancer, by the time I got around to seeing the specialist, had vanished!

John 14:27 "Peace I leave with you, My peace I give you. I do not give to you as the world gives. Do not let your hearts be troubled, do not be afraid."

My stress levels are much less – no more drinks after work and I eat food that's healthy.

Proverbs 3:9, 10. "Honour the Lord with your wealth, with the first fruits of all your crops. Then your barns will be filled to overflowing".

No more rushing about and still being late for everything, – I sleep well, rise early and spend the first and the best of my day in prayer and reading His Word - just because I want and need to spend that time with Him. Matthew 28:20 "And surely I am with you always even unto the end of the age".

But best and most amazing of all I don't have that feeling it's all down to me, and all about me. I am not alone, my Father in heaven loves, hears me, comforts me; my Saviour forgives me, strengthens me, changes me, the Holy Spirit teaches me, guides me, nudges me to do what is right, points my attention to Jesus, and what pleases Him.

I joined the prayer group that prayed for me that day after telling my friend that sort of thing just wasn't for me – I'm much too practical and scientific? I discovered the joy of praising God, the wonder of reading his word and the encouragement of sharing faith with others. Since then I have attended Life in the Spirit and got baptised in the Holy Spirit. I have also done the Alpha course and I will tell anyone who will listen and those who won't about the grace and love of our Lord. He knows me and I really want to know Him.

I am only just beginning to understand grace - I have been given peace, joy, healing, forgiveness and so much more – salvation and eternal life.

A wise young man of faith told me that when Jesus moves in He doesn't just shift the furniture around he tears down the house and sets about building Himself a mansion. I know this is true – I've been a counsellor, I know about behaviour modification and I am not this good at it! What I have experienced is His personal transformation. So I guess that this sign around my neck means "Under Construction" and hopefully it will be a long project - the rest of my life.

Oh and although I've been talking about my experience, this is not my story. It is a story of our God, His love, His grace, His amazing, unmerited favour.

The gospel of John says it best (3:16) "For God so loved the world that He gave His one and only Son that whoever believes in Him would not perish but have everlasting life."

This friend of mine has grown in the Lord by leaps and bounds and is one of the leaders at her church. What an amazing story of grace.

With God all things are possible and God Himself declared this in Jeremiah 32v 27, 'Behold, l am the God of all flesh. Is there anything that is too hard for me?' No one is beyond redemption and no one is too hard for God.

Go on, order salvation for your family too.

CHAPTER 2

HINTS AND TIPS ON HOW TO PRAY FOR OUR FAMILIES TO BE SAVED

I have used these tips to pray for my family but that does not mean that this is a formula on how we should pray for our loved ones. You can use my tips on how to pray or ask God to give you yours. What matters is that you pray the will of the Father and that is all that matters.

1. Have their photo with you when you pray if you cannot lay hands on them. Pray over the photo and talk to them in the photo e.g. John my son God loves and I love you too and I pray for your Salvation. Lord let your Grace be upon John and be with him wherever he is right now. This must be done every time you have the opportunity to pray for a loved one. This cannot be a one off thing remember Jesus said to pray without ceasing.
2. Go in their bedroom while they are not there (make sure you do not get caught). Pray for that family member for their salvation touch their pillows and pray that as they lay their head on that pillow God will touch them.
3. Pray for their clothes. What a great way to do laundry! While you have your family member's clothes in your hands ready for ironing

or washing pray that God will reveal Himself to them as they put on those clothes. Pray that each time they put on those clothes they make good decisions in their lives.

4. Pray in their car that God will direct them each time they go out in that car. Cover the car with the blood of Jesus. Pray for the people who will sit in the car (friends) to be good influence to your family member. Pray over their wigs (Mainly for us Africans) and hair extensions that when they put them on they also put on Christ, humility, love and meekness.

5. Does your family member have a drinking problem? Here is a trick. Get hold of the can of beer in the fridge and pray that God will destroy the desire for alcohol in your family member. By the way I am not saying that this would be their last drink but you never know what God can do. Giving your family member lecture on the dangers of drinking will by no means change them but praying for God's grace over their life to help them to stop drinking is the only way to go if you want lasting and genuine change. Our motto as parents or spouses should be 'pressure to God and love to the family'. There you go! Do not put pressure on people but rather put pressure on God until he hears you.

Luke 18v1-8, 'Then He spoke a parable to them, that men always ought to pray and not lose heart, ² saying: "There was in a certain city a judge who did not fear God nor regard man. ³ Now there was a widow in that city; and she came to him, saying, 'Get justice for me from my adversary.' ⁴ And he would not for a while; but afterward he said within himself, 'Though I do not fear God nor regard man, ⁵ yet because this widow troubles me I will avenge her, lest by her continual coming she weary me.'"

⁶ Then the Lord said, "Hear what the unjust judge said. ⁷ And shall God not avenge His own elect who cry out day and night to Him, though He bears long with them? ⁸ I tell you that He will avenge

them speedily. Nevertheless, when the Son of Man comes, will He really find faith on the earth?"

The moral of the parable is be persistent, do not lose heart and have faith that whatever you are asking God to do, He will perform it in the fullness of time.

6. Do not generalise when you pray for your loved ones. Mention them by name and pray what you want from God for them. A friend of mine from high school told me how she started praying for her daughter's wedding day and marriage from the day she was born. I know this may sound ridiculous and overzealous but God gives us the desires of our hearts and even if we die before we see some of the things we prayed for our loved ones, God will still remember those prayers we banked ages ago. That is how we bank prayers in the kingdom of God. (By the way my friend's daughter just recently got married! Yes the same one whose mother prayed for when she was a baby just got married. He is faithful isn't He?). Pray for your child's future spouse that the person will be the one your child loves, the one who loves your child too and above all the one who loves God. Even if you do not see an evangelist in your future son in law (the boy your daughter is dating) persevere in prayer. Some evangelists never looked like they would stand on the pulpit when they first started! All I am saying is do not judge the people your loved ones are dating because the grace of God is for all of us to enjoy.

When I walked into the Chifamba family I am sure my in laws must have thought, 'Lord what is this?' They obviously had prayed for a daughter in law who loves God but guess what they got? A demon possessed girl who was going to church just so I could impress them. They must have been disheartened and must have questioned God. I was the opposite of what they had asked for. I looked older than their son (or even older than my mother in law!!!). I was not anywhere near their expectations but isn't God faithful? Look at me now. I am certainly not the best daughter in law they have but I am saved, delivered and completely changed. Na na na to the devil! So do not despair if some of the people who show up on your door step are far from what you expected because our God is the God of all flesh. Nothing is too hard for Him. He will change that person into exactly what you desire or even better than what you desire. Some people are assigned to our destiny for a reason and for a purpose.

Having said that, it does not mean we should not pray against some relationships in our children's lives because some of them are definitely a counterfeit from the enemy. If you feel some alarm bells going or you are not at peace with the relationships, the best way to pray in situations like that is, God if he or she is not the one for my child let this relationship end now in the name of Jesus. It is ok to pray like that. You are not being judgemental; you are seeking God's wisdom.

7. Pray the word of God for them. Why invent your own prayers when you can pray the word of God back to Him. Praying the scriptures to God is like standing in a court of law with evidence of the case you are presenting. Like Mrs Eunor Guti once said, 'It's like taking a mirror and showing it to God, so He can see Himself in the mirror.' The teaching from Mrs Guti in 2004 really impacted my life. Ever since I heard her teaching on praying the scriptures for our children, I have not stopped doing that because I have seen how faithful God is to his word. God said in His word that He Himself is servant of his own word.

(NKJV) Psalms 138 v 2 says,

'I will worship toward Your holy temple,

And praise Your name

For Your loving kindness and Your truth;

For You have magnified Your word above all Your name.'

Take note of the last sentence. God has made Himself servant of His own word. He bows down to His word. So what does that mean Salome? I am glad you asked!

What is means is when we pray the word of God back to him we are praying the will of the Father and He is faithful to His word so He will do as He says in His word. Prayer is asking God to do what He has promised in His word. God says in His word that He will not let His word come back to Him void, but it will have to accomplish that which it was assigned to do first.

Isaiah 55v10-11New King James Version (NKJV) says,

'For as the rain comes down, and the snow from heaven,

And do not return there,

But water the earth,

And make it bring forth and bud,

That it may give seed to the sower

And bread to the eater,

[11] So shall My word be that goes forth from My mouth;

It shall not return to Me void,

But it shall accomplish what I please,

And it shall prosper *in the thing* for which I sent it.'

This verse makes me excited. I do not have to make up my own prayers, I just ask according to the word of God. So here are some of the prayers I make for my family and myself.

I always pray that as a family we grow strong in the spirit increase in wisdom and stature and find favour with God and with people. (Luke 2 v52).

I also pray that my children are taught by God and great will be their peace. (Isaiah 54v13).

I pray that my children are blessed, that they are known among the gentiles, and that all who see them acknowledge them and say they are the posterity whom the Lord has blessed, (Isaiah 61v9).

I do not know how many times I have repeated that prayer to God. God is faithful to His word and I do not know how many times I can say this to convince you my friend to do this every day. I have seen it in my children many times. I will never forget when my youngest daughter was in grade one or two; I went to see her teacher for parent teacher interviews. The teacher talked to me about how our daughter was going at school. Just as I was about to leave the teacher asked if it was ok for her to ask something personal and I said I was ok with that. I started to worry a bit because I was not sure where this was going. I thought my daughter was in trouble.

The teacher asked, 'Mrs Chifamba I just want to let you know that I am really touched by the way your daughter prays. The way she does it makes me wonder where she gets that from because it is really touching. How come she is like that?' Now that changed my worry to excitement in less than two seconds! I could not believe that a teacher was moved by a little girl's prayers. I went on to tell the teacher that it is the power of the Holy Spirit and only He could get the glory. I explained that the Holy Spirit helps us to pray as we should. That made the teacher very hungry for some more so she asked if she could come for prayers when we did healing services at church. I gladly told her that she was welcome to do that, which she did. The following Sunday that teacher was there at church being prayed over to be filled with the Holy Spirit. God is faithful; He made my children to be known among the people as He promises in His word. God can use our children to reach out to other people.

One day we went to our youngest daughter's school assembly. It was the last one as she finished year 12 in 2017. She got 3 awards at the assembly and the principal stopped us briefly before we left and said to us, 'you must be very proud parents 'and we thanked him and the staff at the school for all their hard work. We were indeed very proud parents. As if that was not enough one of the parents stopped us soon after we finished talking to the principal and said to us, 'are you by any chance Rumbi's parents?' Rumbi is our middle child. We gladly said yes but we were not sure where that was going. The lady then said, 'I work with your daughter at the hospital and I just wanted to let you know that your daughter is a renowned nurse. 'She went on and on explaining what she meant and I tell you we were very proud parents.

Hints And Tips On How To Pray For Our Families To Be Saved

In 2017 our youngest daughter registered for the Miss Universe Australia. She told us she had prayed about it and asked God for guidance, so she was sure God was guiding her in this. To be honest I was not very enthusiastic about it at first because I really wanted her to focus more

on her studies. Anyway she got into the competition as one of the South Australian State finalists, and we all started supporting her with prayers and fund raising. Other girls were raising a lot of money and hers was slowly growing. The day for the State finals came and we all got ready. Our daughter went earlier to the venue for interviews and we joined the girls who were competing at six in the evening. As soon as we walked in, I noticed that the other girls who were competing were all wearing very stunning dresses and my daughter's outfit was ok but not as glamorous. Knowing how much the other girls had raised and what the other girls were wearing, my faith started to dwindle in no time at all.

God has promised us that 'our children will be known among the people and all who see them will acknowledge them that they are the posterity whom the Lord has blessed.' I will cut a long story short. After my faith had started going down, one of the judges came to me and said very good things about my daughter. That was the injection I needed to boost my faith again. Our daughter was chosen to be one of the finalists to represent South Australia at a national level. It was in the paper two days later.

What is that? God being faithful to His word. He promised us that our children shall be known among the people and everyone will acknowledge that they are blessed people. When we pray the word back to God, He will honour His word.

I pray that we seek the kingdom of God first and His righteousness. Matthew 6v33.

I pray that Jesus teaches us how to pray and how to give and how to meditate on His word. We have to believe as we pray that God is able to do as He says in His word. Imagine asking God to teach you how to dwell in Him! When you ask that you are guaranteed fruit, then you can ask what you desire and it shall be done for you. Check John 15v1-8. Most of us want to rush to asking what we desire but do not want to spend time with God as Jesus asked us to do. The idea is to meditate on his word, speak it in faith but also to do just as it says in the word. If we do according to the word of God we are guaranteed success in all areas of our lives including our families.

Joshua1v8, God told Joshua what to do to get success in his life.

'This Book of the Law shall not depart from your mouth, but you shall meditate in it day and night, that you may observe to do according to all that is written in it. For then you will make your way prosperous, and then you will have good success.' The mistake we make is we pray for success and prosperity and we write that down every year on our prayer lists for us and our families, but we never pray that God helps us to mediate on His word and do according to His word. No wonder we end up giving up; we think God does not answer our prayers but we do not want to do what has to be done to get success.

If you read Deuteronomy 28v1-14, it is very easy to get all caught up in the blessings that we forget to focus on the first statement of the promise. My friend let us pray that we listen to God's word and do as it says, then God has promised us that blessings will even overtake us.!!!!. We will be the head and not the tail, above only and not beneath. We will lend and not borrow. Read the whole chapter for yourself my friend. It is jam packed with promises that will overtake us when we do according to the Word of God.

Let us pray that as families, we learn to give. The promise is that when we give, we will receive a reward. We do not need to pray for the rewards but when we give, sure enough God will fulfil his word. Luke 6v38.

Let us pray that our children will honour us, so that all will go well with them. Friend, I could go on and on but my prayer is you get into the word of God, study it, meditate on it, do as it says and pray it for yourself and for your loved ones. Prayer then becomes easy. Study the word, believe it and pray it back to God.

Let us also pray that God would send preachers to our family members as the word says in Romans10v13-15;

'For "whoever calls on the name of the Lord shall be saved."

How then shall they call on Him in whom they have not believed? And how shall they believe in Him of whom they have not heard? And how shall they hear without a preacher? And how shall they preach unless they are sent? As it is written:

"How beautiful are the feet of those who preach the gospel of peace. Who bring glad tidings of good things?"

See, Paul here is reasoning with us that how can our family members who are lost call upon the name of the Lord unless someone tells them about Jesus. These days there are so many fake prophets and healers who are confusing people with lies. At the end of the day, people do not know who to believe. That is why we have to pray that God sends the right people to our loved ones who will tell them the truth about God, so they can be saved and start calling upon the name of the Lord.

Here is a motto that works in our church, 'Put pressure on God and love people'. We got this from Luke 18v1-8

'Then He spoke a parable to them, that men always ought to pray and not lose heart, ² saying: "There was in a certain city a judge who did not fear God nor regard man. ³ Now there was a widow in that city; and she came to him, saying, 'Get justice for me from my adversary.' ⁴ And he would not for a while; but afterward he said within himself, 'Though I do not fear God nor regard man, ⁵ yet because this widow troubles me I will avenge her, lest by her continual coming she weary me."

⁶ Then the Lord said, "Hear what the unjust judge said. ⁷ And shall God not avenge His own elect who cry out day and night to Him, though He bears long with them? ⁸ I tell you that He will avenge them speedily. Nevertheless, when the Son of Man comes, will He really find faith on the earth?"

The unjust judge had to solve this widow's problem not because he feared God or he was just, but because the widow kept pressuring him to do it. No one likes to be pressured to do things and no one wants to be nagged. The widow in the story knew how to get to the unjust judge.

She kept nagging him until he did it for her. She could have given up at the first no but she did not take no for an answer, so she kept on asking.

Jesus is teaching us here that instead of wearing our family and friends down, telling them how they should run their lives, we should keep praying for them until God answers our prayers. This is not to say God will not say no to our requests sometimes especially if they are not in His will, but we are being taught here to be persistent in our prayers. If we are praying the will of God in our lives and in the lives of others, God will answer our prayers. The moral of the story is, do not give up praying for people and circumstances to change.

Isaiah 62 v 1 teaches us the same idea of not giving up in prayer.

'For Zion's sake I will not hold My peace,

And for Jerusalem's sake I will not rest,

Until her righteousness goes forth as brightness,

And her salvation as a lamp *that* burns.

The prophet is saying I will not keep quiet until see change .I will not rest in prayer until I see God restore what the enemy destroyed.

Again in verses 6 -7 it says,

'I have set watchmen on your walls, O Jerusalem;

They shall never hold their peace day or night.

You who make mention of the Lord, do not keep silent,

⁷ And give Him no rest till He establishes

And till He makes Jerusalem a praise in the earth.

We are encouraged to call upon the Lord day and night and not to lecture people day and night. Sometimes we parents want to get in there and fix our kids by talking to them and lecturing them (nothing wrong with giving advice), but we are encouraged to spend time with God if we want to see change in our kids or any situation in life. I am guilty of wanting to put pressure on people to change but the more I pressurise them, the more they do the opposite. I have learnt the hard way that the word of God still stands. We have to put pressure on God and leave all our situations in God's hands. It is God we have to talk to day and night, not people. Ladies let us get this straight. Giving your husband a lecture to change will not work but praying for him day and night will definitely work (husbands too should take note of this). Do not give God rest! In other words, put pressure on God and He will hear your prayers because He is faithful to His word.

All the promises of God are a yes and amen in Jesus for the glory of our God, 2 Corinthians1v20.

CHAPTER 3

SCROLL DOWN THE MENU TO DELIVERANCE

Maybe your story is a bit complicated. You not only messed up but you are driven by a force beyond you. Maybe you conjured up spirits of the dead through ancestral worship and you have worshipped other gods. You know of course that there is only one God but you have been told there are many ways of getting to Him and that got you into so much trouble. Maybe you do not sleep well at all and you do not have peace. You are most probably sick all the time and you have been told it is because you are not pleasing the dead enough, so you need to do some more. You feel scared and worried that if you abandon these spirits, you will be dead. You have seen others go down to the pit for playing games with these spirits and you feel there is no way out. You hear voices that no one else hears in your home and everyone thinks you are nuts. Your marriage is not working because these spirits will not share you with your spouse. One minute you love your spouse then the next minute you think you made a mistake to marry that person.

Like Paul says in Romans 7 v15, "For what I am doing, I do not understand. For what I will to do, that I do not practise; but what I hate, that I do." Hey that is frustrating, the good you want to say you do not say but the bad stuff. Does that sound familiar? You are trying so hard to keep at least one genuine friend but they all seem to notice something you do not see yourself and they drift away.

At work you get blamed for just about everything. No one notices the good that you do but only the few mistakes you make are blown out of proportion, and look very bad. You go to New Age people who seem to be very nice people. Surely they do not want to do you any harm but their source of power is a bit weird, although it looks like it works. The devil does not do the wrong to get you into his tricks. Sometimes he does some things that really look like it is all for your own good but trust me, 'been there done that' the devil is a liar.

Maybe you think someone can help by telling you the future, that way you are prepared for it. The fortune teller even knows your name and address before you even say anything to him or her, surely that cannot be wrong! You are desperate for a way out and you know that church will not help because you have attended church once and nothing happened. You do feel helpless now. You feel let down by friends, because the more you share your problems, the more they drift away. You earn good money at work but you do not seem to be getting anywhere at all in terms of progress. You have had enough of this life and you have got no idea what can help. Do not get depressed my friend, the way out is available in God.

You have tried Reiki for help but you seem to be going around in circles. You have looked at the horoscopes but that has not given you any hope at all, just a false sense of security. You have been involved in new age but not much has changed in your life. You have never stopped talking to the dead, especially your dear grandmother who used to help you whenever you got into trouble when she was alive and now that she has passed on, she does not seem to help. What could possibly go wrong with talking to nana who was always there for you? Maybe it is your late mum or dad you are talking to. You love them so much and you feel there is nothing wrong with talking to them. Believe me my friend, the devil is a trickster. He can pretend to be your departed loved one and all he would like you to do is open the door for him.

You have even asked for help from your neighbour who is a white witch because she seems to have it all worked out but that has yielded nothing for you. By the way, you have been told that white witches are ok by your friend and to look out only for the black ones. Well, allow me to be blunt here my friend, a witch is a witch. Nana is gone now, she is with the Lord, so you do not need to talk to her. The bible forbids that in Deuteronomy 18 v 10-14. It is a no no talking to the dead or practising witchcraft. Mum or dad are gone too, so we cannot talk to them either even though the temptation is high. Horoscopes are forbidden big time in the bible.

Deuteronomy 18 v 9-14 says, 'When you come into the land which the Lord your God is giving you, you shall not learn to follow the abominations of those nations. [10] There shall not be found among you *anyone* who makes his son or his daughter pass through the fire, *or one* who practices witchcraft, *or* a soothsayer, or one who interprets omens, or a sorcerer, [11] or one who conjures spells, or a medium, or a spiritist, or one who calls up the dead. [12] For all who do these things *are* an abomination to the Lord, and because of these abominations the Lord your God drives them out from before you. [13] You shall be blameless before the Lord your God. [14] For these nations which you will dispossess listened to soothsayers and diviners; but as for you, the Lord your God has not appointed such for you.'

Friend, how clear can the word of God be? I think this explains everything we need to hear about the world of darkness and its practises.

You kind of know there is something wrong with these practises but you know no other solution to your problems. Well, I have good news for you; do not walk out of that restaurant before you order what is called 'Deliverance.' It is there on the menu, just scroll down after salvation. There is deliverance just waiting to be ordered and again it is for free. The Man who does the deliverance is none other than the Lord Jesus Himself. Jesus Himself, by His own mouth declared that if He sets a man free, he is free indeed. John 8v36 "therefore if the Son makes you free, you shall be free indeed." How good is that! You do not have to doubt if you are saved or not. Jesus does a good job. When He starts something, He finishes and the apostle Paul summed it up in Philippians 1v6 "being confident of this very thing, that He who has begun a good work in you will complete it until the day of Jesus Christ."

I will take you to a man who was in a big mess in the bible, being tormented by evil powers and he was even called Legion (which was not his real name but because he was possessed by that many spirits, they called him Legion). No one could help him, he was unapproachable and if he was chained, he would break the chains. He lived among the tombs and his family most probably had given up on him. By today's language, the man had a mental problem so he needed to be in an institution and highly likely on a very heavy dose of drugs to calm him down. Doctors would have explained to his family that they had to accept his situation and rely on drugs, which seems to be a very sensible thing to do. Counselling would have been encouraged in today's world but back in those days there were no counsellors and if they were there, no one mentioned them.

That man was in a big mess and he seemed to have been beyond any help anyone could offer. Here he was, still in his mess, screaming his head off as usual and being quite violent when the Master Himself showed up on the scene. As soon as Jesus walked towards him, the demons recognised Him and they started screaming and begging to be left alone or to go into the head of swine nearby. Jesus commanded the demons to leave the man and they did. Wow, what a dramatic change of life the man had. From being a mentally challenged man to a preacher in less than a day (because Jesus told him to go and tell the world what God had done for him). The bible tells us how that man went everywhere declaring what the Lord had done for him. What an amazing story of deliverance!

The Bible makes it so clear that Jesus is above all principalities and friend, let us stand on that word and call on His name and you and I will be set free. Jesus commanded us Christians to lay hands on the sick and to cast out demons in His name and by the way, it is only through His name that we are to cast out demons. Check Mark chapter 16 v 15-18 and you will see that demons should never torment us at all because there is a name that is above all names, by which we can be delivered.

If you think that is your problem and you are wondering how and where to get help, you might need to go to a bible based church and walk in there and ask for help. It took a very serious sickness for me to realise that I was in trouble and what I thought was culture, was actually destroying my life.

So when I got saved by the grace of God I realised what my family and I were into and I decided to stay out of it all. I now know that some of our cultural beliefs are not of God. This is not easy to explain to family and I must say I could have tried to be polite to my family while I tried to explain myself, but I did some damage in my family relationships. I thought that I had to say it in such a way that no one would then have to try and convince me again to go back to those things. Well here is one area I needed immediate help from God, my mouth. I got very arrogant and hurt some family members. Anyway to cut a long story short, relationships have been healed now and everyone in the family respects my faith. Family members are being saved one by one, for with God all things are possible.

Let me help someone here. Getting away from these cultural things can cause a lot of trouble with family but, "if God is for us who can be against us?" the bible says. I was delivered from the powers of darkness after having nearly lost my life and my marriage but thanks be to God, I now have life and life more abundantly as Jesus said in John 10v10. The last time I checked, I am still 100 per cent African but a Christian one and indeed the Lord set me free and I am free indeed.

Well, Salome you do not know my life. I am married to the eldest boy in the family and when they do these rituals I have to be there otherwise I will get into trouble with my husband, remember the bible says to be submissive? Well, my sister let me say this to you, with God all things are possible. Many women find it the hardest to come out in the open about their faith, especially in the Shona culture, but I have good news. Do not panic at all, God will be there 24/7 to help. Pray about this and fast and see what God can do. He will do wonders I must say. So look out for religions who say there are other ways to the Father. They are not of God because the only way to the Father is through His Son Jesus and that is the truth, not a Western idea. It is a John 14 v 6 Jesus idea!

With family not being able to understand your new life, you need to learn this dear friend that God wants us to continue as a family and to love one another. The bible says to speak the truth in love. We still have to take our stance on our beliefs, let everyone know where we stand in our faith but saying it in love. I wish I had known this ages ago because I said things I regretted later on in life which I could have avoided. Do not argue with anyone in the family. Start saying positive things about them and speak life into their world, after all we are saved by grace and never worked out our own salvation. Praise God for them, even if you can not see a hint of change. One day God will reward you if you do not give up on any one of your family members.

Remember Joshua and the walls of Jericho. Read the whole story. It is an inspiring story of how effective praise is, especially before you see a change in anyone. Thank God for that sister in law who gives you heartache because of your faith. Thank God for your father in-law who does not want to see you going to church. Start thanking God for the man of God in your house, even if you do not see him getting off the drink and changing his abusive behaviour.

Thank God for that son of yours who has been on drugs for years. Go on, tell the Lord how much you thank Him for your daughter who will not speak to you because you took the grand kids to church one day and she got mad at you. It does not make sense to praise God in such situations but just like Paul and Silas in Prison in Acts 16, sing songs to God in any situation and see if He will not cause the most exciting prison break ever!

Look, there is power in praise and if it worked for Paul and Silas, it will work for us too. Every morning before you start judging any one, thank God for your family. Give the enemy a nervous breakdown when you do that! Jesus promised us that it will not be easy being a Christian. He did not promise us a rose garden. So go on fellow Christian, wage the war against the enemy and praise your God for things not yet seen and see how God will set an ambush against the enemy. Remember the story of Jehoshaphat in the Old Testament. He praised God when three huge armies came to attack him and while he and his people were praising, God set an ambush against the enemy. The enemies ended up killing each other. By the way, the battle is not yours but God's, that is what the bible says.

The only thing we should never do as Christians is to compromise our faith to please family and friends. Actually, family and friends will be watching to see if you will give in and do something contrary to your faith. So hold on to your faith and never give in at all.

So ask for deliverance, it is on the menu, order it now for free. It comes with the package. Christianity is not about do's and don'ts. It is not about rules and regulations so that if you break one of them you are out. What God asks us not to do is for our protection and not to deprive us of the pleasures of this world.

For a start, when God said not to talk to the dead He was not saying that to prevent us from loving our dearly departed. What happens is the enemy waits for an opening so he can bring in lots of things to attack us. It is very tempting to talk to our loved ones who are gone, especially soon after they are gone. I felt the same when I lost my mum. In Deuteronomy 18 from verse 9 onwards, God forbids us from any communication with the dead. He says He forbids us to be like '—one who conjures spells, or a medium, or a spiritist, or one who calls up the dead. For all those who do such things are an abomination to the Lord'. Let us agree on this one. We are not to call on the dead and the dead are all the people who are not alive today.

It does not matter if these people were Christians or not, we do not talk to the dead and I think this is quite clear. Well, Salome what about that pastor who was such a great man of God? Surely he is with the Lord? No! We cannot talk to him either. Let us say God said no to even the most anointed of them all. We do not talk to the dead regardless of what they did here on earth, not even the patriarchs in the bible or any man or woman who did great works for God. The only way to the Father was narrowed down to only one and that is through His Son Jesus: John 14 v6 '----no one comes to the Father except through me.' There are no other ways to the Father for us Christians and that is what is in the bible. We cannot hide this truth. God is not being unfair by saying the only way to Him is through His Son, but He is protecting us from counterfeits.

We do not worship Angels although they are heavenly beings and we also do not talk to them either. One of the Angels in Revelations was talking to John and John thought to honour the Angel by falling down and worshipping him. The angel was quick to correct that in Revelations 22v9, 'Then he said to me see that you do not do that. For I am your fellow servant and of your brethren the prophets, and of those who keep the words of this book. Worship God'. See? The angels do not like being worshipped so let us not disappoint them. Yes, God has sent angels to speak to people, so it's just forbidden to pray to them because they are not part of the Godhead. Prayer is talking to God so if we are not talking to Him but people and angels then that is not prayer. Paul in Colossians 2 v 20 forbids the worshipping of angels too. Yes angels of the Lord make a hedge around us, the bible says that but please let us not pray to them because the bible forbids this practice.

Horoscopes are not of God, therefore fellow Christian do not check on what your star says from now on. Are you disappointed? Well, in this relationship with God, He wants all the glory and honour; trust me, He deserves it. He even admits that He is a jealous God. We do not do these things because we are worried that God will punish us but because we love God so much and we want to make Him happy. I am faithful in my relationship with my husband not because I do not want to get divorced but because I love him and him alone. I do not have to think twice about this because this is a love relationship so it should be the same in our relationship with God.

There are some things that we should not watch even on TV because the enemy can use anything to get you into trouble. Do not watch psychic shows or ghost shows as well as shows on witchcraft. Pornographic movies are equally bad. Please pray to God to help you get out of addictions to pornography or TV shows with bad themes and ask God to help you out of those internet programmes that are not of God. The enemy uses these to open doors to attack you.

So go on, ask God to deliver you free of charge.

CHAPTER 4

Healing Is On The Menu; Therefore It Is In The Kitchen

The world today is stressed by a lot of things but the most stressful of them all I think is sickness. When a family member is diagnosed with a terminal sickness or when they are just not well, that can plunge us into stress beyond us. It is even more devastating when it is us who are sick. You want to get well and go back to work or go about your normal daily routines in life but being in a hospital bed for two weeks is something that can drive you crazy. I do not like being sick and I think no one likes that either, but we do not have control over these things in life.

While you are in that restaurant you have already made up your mind that you are going to order salvation and deliverance, now you are looking down the menu and the word healing stands out. You maybe have come here to have a break from looking after your spouse or parent who is not well. You want to just have a quick meal so you can go back home and look after maybe your child who has been ill for a while and you cannot stand looking at your child sick all the time.

Maybe you are the one who is not well. Indigestion! The pain is shocking after meals, especially at night. You cannot enjoy certain foods but you still cannot control the pain. The Doctor has prescribed antacids and much more but still you are not getting anywhere. You have been through many tests but nothing is wrong with you, the Doctor said. That is stressing you because you want the results to say something so the Doctors can get to it!

That sore back that you have had for years is a sign all is not well. Maybe you still have not realised that you have got inner pain in your heart that the Doctors cannot see. After that painful divorce you have been having this back ache. Pain in the heart cannot be treated by a medical Doctor. The best they can do is put you on Valium so you can sleep well. Well we cannot blame the Doctors because they cannot heal broken hearts.

Maybe you are not divorced but your children are giving you a hard time. They do not want to talk to you or your husband. You cannot see the grandkids because your kids are angry with you and they have not told you why. Maybe it is not the kids but you were abused when you were little and you did not tell anyone in your family because the person who did that to you is a dear member of the family. You cannot forgive that family member and I do not blame you. That is the reason why you cannot eat properly or sleep very well at night.

Maybe a death in the family has left you scarred for life and you cannot get over the grieving process and you feel so alone. Maybe you have been a victim of segregation at work and you lost your job and since then, you cannot sleep properly.

Physical pain can be a result of all sorts of things that happened to us a long time ago. I have nothing against going to the doctors because they can be used by God to heal us. There are times when we know deep down in our hearts that we are sick because we are hurting inside. This is where I think it is hard for a medical doctor to prescribe anything at all.

Things like ulcers, indigestion, back pain, chronic headaches, arthritis, eating disorders, high blood pressure and many more conditions can be a result of past hurts or the current hurts in our lives. I am not a doctor as you can tell but all I am saying is in many cases people who suffer from these things, as soon as they get inner healing, instantly get healed from the other conditions.

Well Salome, if you are not a medical doctor how do you know these things? From experience! My mum suffered from high blood pressure and I believe hers was a result of family issues she had no control over. She used to share a lot with us (her kids) and we all knew why she had high blood pressure. She was then on medication since 1972 and I do not blame that woman for feeling hurt. We prayed with her for a long time and I believe she received her healing and she is in a better place now.

By the way, her death gave me stomach pains that I could not handle and I questioned God while at the same time wanting to look very strong to the world. I went before God and really told Him that I was not a strong Christian (which he knew anyway) and that I could not cope and I needed Him to heal my broken heart. I must confess, I started to feel better so much that I did not have to take Mylanta every night.

I also had issues with my Dad and being a child I could not do anything, though I tried many times to fight with him. Everyone in the family used to tell me off about this including my mother (I thought I was doing mum a favour by lashing out at dad but I was making my mum angry too) but that did not stop me wanting to get even with my father. I wanted him to be like the fathers I read about in books who were perfect. I do not know why I wanted him to be perfect, because I was not a perfect daughter to him! I had to learn that I have to respect my father no matter what because that is what the bible says. I ended up going to my father and asking for forgiveness from him for the way I used to speak to him and sometimes treat him. Well he is human and he is my father and God by His Grace has helped me to love and forgive my father. Now you see why I know that inner or emotional pain can cause physical pain, **been there done that!**

If we look in the bible, Jesus' ministry was all about healing and restoration. In John 10v10 Jesus said, 'the thief comes not only to kill but to steal and destroy but I came that you may have life and life more abundantly.' See my friend we all know what the thief, the devil does. He destroys relationships, he makes us hurt and not forgive, we get sick and depressed because that is what the enemy wants in our lives but the good news is Jesus came, that you and I can have life and life more abundantly.

Like I have already mentioned, if you invite Jesus into your heart He takes over and helps you to heal because he is the healer Himself. Matthew 3v23-24 talks about how Jesus went about in Galilee preaching the gospel of the kingdom and healing all manner of sickness. There is a healer and that is Jesus and I can tell you there is no sickness greater than Him, there is no relationship too broken to mend and there is no heart too broken for Jesus to heal.

When Jesus came back from the wilderness after forty days and forty nights of prayer and fasting, He then immediately started His ministry. One day He went into the synagogue and was given the scroll to read and He read Isaiah 61. Jesus stood up and read that passage of scripture in Luke 4 v 18-24 and He sat down and the bible says all eyes were on Him. And without fear and hesitation, Jesus announced His mission statement. To heal the broken hearted, to preach good news to the poor, to open prison doors for those who are bound and to proclaim the year of jubilee of our Lord. Then He said the famous sentence, "Today this scripture has been fulfilled in your midst" meaning I am the One who Isaiah was talking about. That did not impress His people but who cares! Jesus is the One who can heal the broken heart. So today, like Jesus said, the scripture is fulfilled in Him. He is the One who can set us free from the prisons of our lives. He is the One who can open prison doors for us. Check Psalms 147 v 3 again it talks about God healing the broken hearted. He is the only One who can bind up your bleeding heart if you just ask Him to. Tell Him how much you are hurting right now and He will heal your heart.

One thing I have to mention is, this healing of physical and emotional pain is also free. Jesus does not want you to do anything to deserve it. Just come to Him as you are. That is right, you do not have to clean your act first. Come as you are. Still not sure, or not very keen to forgive? He will help you. Remember Christ came to save the lost not the righteous. He is even willing to leave 99 sheep unattended to look for one lost sheep!! In the world of economics that does not make sense. No one wants to risk 99.9% of their wealth but in the kingdom of heaven, God is willing to leave the 99 unattended just to find that one lost and stray sheep. Find a church where they believe in the word of God and in the power of the Holy Spirit and be part of that community so the brethren can help you to grow and heal.

The bible tells us that Jesus bore our pain and our shame on the cross. Isaiah 53 v5 says, "By His stripes we are healed" and note the job is already done on the cross so you do not have to do anything to earn God's love.

Place your hand where you are hurting. If it is in your heart just put your hand on your chest. Let us agree, you and I, that our God can heal you today. Remember what Jesus said when He stood up in the synagogue to read the scroll in Luke 4 v 18 – 22. He said that TODAY this scripture has been fulfilled. Today, not tomorrow so here is what you and I will do. Let us agree that today the scripture is fulfilled in your life. Lay your hand where you need healing and we will pray together. Or if it is not you who is sick, lay your hand on that family member or friend. You say this prayer with me.

Father, in the name of Jesus. (By the way, that name is the only password for heaven. If you use any other name you will not be logged in. Heavenly computers have only one user name and password that is, Jesus. John 14v6). So keep going with me, Father in the name of Jesus, I pray today that as you become my Lord and Saviour, you will take away my pain as you say in your word. By your stripes Lord Jesus I am healed and I believe today that you are healing me. You, pain in my body, I command you to leave right now in the name of Jesus.

Amen.

Friend the bible says every promise in the bible is a yes and amen in Jesus 2 Corinthians 1v20, "for all the promises of God in Him are Yes, and in Him Amen, to the glory of God through us." See in Jesus, every promise of God which includes healing is a yes and amen.

The Apostles of Jesus in the Acts of the Apostles did wonders in the name of Jesus. Thousands and thousands of people were healed just by the apostles laying their hands on the sick or sometimes through handkerchiefs or shadows. Peter just needed to have his shadow on a sick person for them to be healed. Paul used handkerchiefs if he could not get to where the sick were. Yes that happened for real, it is in the bible!

I know what you are probably thinking right now. Where are the miracles today? Here in this life, those miracles are happening and they are still on the menu so you can order your healing today without a doubt. Do not let the enemy make you wonder on how God is going to heal your past or that tumour you have got. Like I said, before you do not have to know how God heals it because no one know how He heals a tumour but all we know is He heals and that is enough to know.

As I have already mentioned before, as the diner in a restaurant, you do not need to see how the kitchen staff prepare the meals. It is good to sit back, relax and leave the rest to the wonderful chefs in the kitchen. After all, that is why it is a restaurant, you are there to be served. With healing you do not have to worry about how God does the healing of a broken heart. Sit back, relax and receive your healing. The Chef's got it all covered!

In 1998 I woke up one day with the worst pain I have ever had in my lower belly. It was worse than labour pains. My husband and I quickly rushed to the emergency where I was told I had an ovarian cyst. I was referred to a specialist who told me that I was to have an operation to remove the cyst. I did not like the whole idea of an operation so I started praying for healing. I asked the doctor if there was another way of removing the cyst and of course there was not, unless the cyst did burst on its own. That got me really interested so I asked the doctor how the cyst could burst on its own and he casually said there were types that burst on their own. Without hesitation I said to the doctor, "can I have the one that bursts on its own please?" The doctor laughed a lot and said to me that we do not choose things like that.

Well a week before the doctor could do the operation, he checked on the cyst again and to his amazement it was getting smaller! He told me that he was going to put the operation on hold and monitor the cyst. Sure enough, after another week the cyst had become so small, the doctor called the operation off. I know that was not a coincidence but the healing power of God. Later on that year, I met a family member who had just had that similar operation I was going to have. The scar from the operation was so big that I just thanked God that I did not have one done.

CHAPTER 5

No Second Thoughts About This One — Ask For The Holy Spirit

I have been to a number of restaurants in my life and experience has taught me that there are some things you just cannot resist on the menu. If you are hungry and I mean really really hungry, you just want to eat and you have to have your main meal. You have to eat if you are hungry. On the other hand, if you are really thirsty, you have to drink. On the menu there is a food item called being filled with the Holy Spirit. Have you heard of that before? Has anyone ever told you how yummy that is and how you cannot just brush that aside? This is a must have for every Christian!

What is that Salome? This is what completes a Christian. The experience of being filled with the Holy Spirit is the most important part of the meal for a Christian. Of course you have to be saved, that is why you are still sitting in that restaurant otherwise by now you would have left. You cannot leave before you order this one. Amazing, fulfilling and much more.

Would you want to order this experience? It's on the menu and you need this experience like you need your next breath.

Well I guess the first question to ask is who is the Holy Spirit? I will do my best to describe Him to you before you can place your order. He is a He by the way, because He is a person. He is part of the Godhead. He is God. Remember God is three persons in one, hence the name Trinity. God is God the Father, God the Son and God the Holy Spirit. The Holy Spirit is part of the Godhead who is with us as Jesus said John 15v26 "But when the Helper comes, whom I shall send to you from the Father, The Spirit of truth who proceeds from the Father He will testify of me." He said that He had to go up so He could come down.

The Holy Spirit has been there since the beginning. In Genesis 1v26 God said, "Let us make man in our own image." That suggests that God the Father was talking to someone other than Himself. He was talking to Jesus and the Holy Spirit. So He has been there right in the beginning and the Bible actually says the Spirit of God hovered upon the face of the earth like a hen would sit on her eggs warming them up to be hatched; Genesis 1v2.

When a kingdom invades a country, they send a governor to the territory or colony to influence the invaded country with the culture of the colonial master. The invading kingdom also sends its own citizens who will work with the governor to influence the culture of the colony they have invaded. The King does not have to be in the colony if the governor is present in the colony. So God's original plan of colonisation in Genesis chapter 1 was to invade earth with Heaven and bring the culture of Heaven on earth with the governor, the Holy Spirit, and the citizens of heaven, us. So that is why God said, "let them have dominion over the earth", meaning us humans to have the kingdom of heaven on earth through dominion on earth. The governor, the Holy Spirit was here on earth ready to work with Adam to influence earth and have dominion but Adam and his wife got cheated out of God's plan by the snake in the Garden of Eden and they fell. They lost dominion, power and authority that they had been given by God for His plan on earth. The Holy Spirit, who is the governor, left and could only come in here and there in the Old Testament.

Then God gave us His Son, the King, in the fullness of time, to bring back the Kingdom, hence the statement, "repent, for the Kingdom of Heaven has arrived" in Mark chapter 1. Jesus then went on to prove what He meant by the Kingdom has arrived as He went about preaching the gospel and healing all manner of sickness. Before His death and resurrection, He had told his disciples that He was going to leave the earth but would come back in a short while. The disciples got very confused because He was saying He was going back to the Father but still coming back. So they asked what he meant by that. Then He explained that He meant the Holy Spirit, the governor of the kingdom of God was coming to replace the King. He even said it was to our advantage that He was going so the Helper could come. Then the governor came on the day of Pentecost to work with the citizens of heaven to influence the earth by bringing the culture of heaven on earth. We are expected to fill the earth with the culture of heaven hence the prayer "Your kingdom come." We cannot influence anyone without the governor working in us and with us. We are here to be filled by the Holy Spirit so we can bring heaven on earth, which is God's plan. So being filled with the Holy Spirit is not an option for us Christians, it is mandatory.

The Holy Spirit is the power that made a virgin girl pregnant. Everyone has heard about the story of Christmas so I do not need to explain in detail who Mary is in the Bible. Well, just in case you haven't heard yet, Mary is the mother of Jesus. This is how she conceived. She was minding her own business waiting for the big day when she would marry her fiancé Joseph. An Angel called Gabriel appeared to her and told her that she was going to have a child and that she should call Him Jesus. The young girl was a bit disturbed but she had to ask the most sensible question she could think of at that time, 'how will this come to pass since I have not known a man?' Good question! Of course, how does a virgin conceive? Well, the Angel had all the details, 'The Holy Spirit will overshadow you therefore what you will conceive shall be called Holy One. That was it and the Angel left before Mary could ask how she was going to tell Joseph. Mary accepted the whole deal with the bravest statement a young Jewish girl, who did not care what this would mean for her reputation, would ever say, 'Let it be according to your will'.

The main focus here is what the angel said, "The Holy Spirit will make you conceive by overshadowing you." So for Jesus to be conceived, the Holy Spirit had to overshadow Mary. Mary was so overshadowed that even when she went to visit Elizabeth her cousin, the mother of John the Baptist, the moment she hugged her, Elizabeth was filled with the Holy Spirit too. Elizabeth started to praise God and to prophecy. Yes that is how infectious the power of the Holy Spirit is. The people we come into contact with will know and feel His presence too. This is the sort of infection I love to catch, not the swine flu or gastro. We can spread this infection if we let the Holy Spirit overshadow us like Mary did.

I can safely say without a shred of doubt that the Holy Spirit is the power that raised Jesus Christ from the dead. Jesus actually died on the cross and was buried by Joseph of Arimathea. On the third day, as we all know, Jesus rose from the dead and He is alive today, otherwise there would not be any good news and we would not be celebrating Easter like we all do. I want to take you back to the tomb where Jesus' body laid motionless, dead. The bible says Jesus actually went and preached to the dead for those three days and went and got the keys of life back from the devil who had grabbed them off of Adam, when he fell in the garden of Eden. So Jesus was very busy in those three days, but let us look at His dead body in the tomb now.

Right, can you imagine the dead body? Ok. The body is cold, motionless and wrapped in cloths as per Jewish custom. A force so powerful comes in and it is so strong that the body starts to move. The body cannot contain the power, it jumps. There! Jesus becomes alive and He takes the cloths off His body and He walks out of the tomb with resurrected power! The power rolls off the stone on the entrance to the tomb and

No Second Thoughts About This One — Ask For The Holy Spirit

Jesus walks out. More like a prison break. He is free and He is alive. That power which raised Christ from the dead is the power of the Holy Spirit; Romans 8v11. In a movie this would be the climax, the part where your adrenalin starts to race, you can easily hear your heart beating in your chest. That power is the one I am talking about and He is free for all of us believers to order.

The Holy Spirit is the promise of the Father to all of us. Salome, isn't that for Pentecostals only? Are you sure you have got it right? Yes I have got it right! The promise is for all of us! I am pretty sure He said for all of us. Let us check the scriptures shall we? In Joel 2 v 28-29 God Himself says, 'Then it shall come to pass afterwards that I will pour out my Spirit upon all flesh. Your sons and your daughters shall prophecy. Your old men shall see visions. And also on My menservants I will pour out my Spirit in those days." Right, does it say on all flesh? Friend, if you have got flesh then God has promised to pour out His Spirit on you. He said he will pour out His Spirit on the young, old men and women. That should cover all the human species. The promise is for all of us.

Well Salome that was for the Jews only, surely God did not mean us the non-Jewish people did He? Let us keep checking the scriptures until we rest our case. On the day of Pentecost when the promise finally came to the apostles and other believers, Peter explained what was happening because people thought they were drunk. First of all, Peter said they were not drunk because it was only 9 o'clock in the morning. He then explained that this was what God had promised through the prophet Joel. He went on to encourage everyone to repent and receive the promise of the Holy Spirit too. Acts 2v39, 'for the promise is to you and to your children, and to all who are afar off, as many as the Lord our God will call.' There! We are all from afar off and God has called you and me so the promise is for us all.

Why should you order this on the menu without fail? Can't someone be a Christian without being filled with the Holy Spirit? Of course NOT! The bible says only those who are led by the Spirit of God are the children of God; Romans 8v14. The bible clearly states that if the Spirit of Christ is not in us we are not His; Romans 8 v 9 '-----Now if anyone does not have the Spirit of Christ, he is not His.' Without the Spirit of God we are lifeless. We are all alive otherwise you would not be reading this book but Jesus clearly stated that He came that we who are alive may have life and life more abundantly; John 10 v 10.

What that means is, there is more to life than just being alive. In Ezekiel 47 there is an analogy of the Holy Spirit as the water flowing from the temple. In verse 9 the bible says, 'And it shall be that every living thing that moves wherever the river goes will live.' When I first read that, I thought I was not seeing right. If living things move then they have life don't they? Let us read this again, 'every living thing that moves wherever the river goes will live.' Mmm interesting isn't it? There must be another level of life which is better than what we know. The Holy Spirit is the living water and Jesus said to drink from Him and we will be satisfied. So whoever is filled by the Spirit of God comes to life, as the scriptures say.

Have you ever felt like you are not satisfied with the things of this world? Have you ever felt empty and without purpose for life? Have you ever thought that if you get more money you will be satisfied then after you had the money you did not feel satisfied at all? Bought a new dress and felt nothing changed? New car and you still feel empty? New house but you are still looking for something more? A new boat maybe? Maybe after you have had kids you thought you would be satisfied. Maybe after the kids have left home you thought you would be so happy?

Let me explain this, a human being is a soul, body and spirit. When we die our bodies decay and our spirits go to heaven. There is eternal life after death. That part which is spirit can only be filled by another spirit and that way we are satisfied. I am not saying a Christian does not have needs, all I am saying is a new car, house, girlfriend or a holiday will not feel that empty void in us. Only the Spirit of God can and that is life more abundantly. If you have a fulfilled life no matter where you are in life, you can still have joy and peace regardless of external circumstances.

Jesus who had a busy schedule to do His Father's business one day took some time to talk to just one woman in John 4. He preached to that woman until she gave her life to God and was changed radically. Jesus emphasised to that woman that those who wanted to worship God had to do it 'In spirit and in truth.' Why? Because God is Spirit, Jesus said. Well if my explanation is not good enough, listen to Jesus please. God is Spirit and people must worship Him in spirit and in truth.

In Romans 8v26, Paul explained to the Romans that we need the Holy Spirit to intercede on our behalf because we do not know how to pray as we should. How great is that! If I do not know what to say in my prayer time, the Spirit prays on my behalf with groans and moans that we do not understand, praying the will of the Father for me. I want the Spirit to help me in my prayer life and He just takes over when I am tired or when I do not know what to say. We all run out of things to say to God sometimes or we do not know how to pray for some things. This is where the Holy Spirit comes in to help and how wonderful is that! We are not left alone to struggle, even in prayer!

Well, are you getting hungry to be filled by the Spirit? So go on, place your order now and that is all for free. Can you believe this? All you need to do is ask. Salome! Don't I need to go to a particular church? No. Go to Jesus, He is the baptiser and it does not matter where you are. Check these scriptures, Matthew 3v11, Luke 3v16, John 1v33. All of them say that Jesus is the one who baptises us with the Holy Spirit. So it is not about a particular place or a particular time of the day, or when you have confessed every sin so much that you feel so holy you do not think you can sin anymore. It is about Jesus baptising you. We fellow Christians can only lay hands on you and ask Jesus to baptise you.

In Acts of the Apostles, the disciples would often lay hands on people to receive the gift of the Spirit and that is the part a fellow Christian can do for you. Acts 19v6, 'When Paul had laid hands on them, the Holy Spirit came upon them, and they spoke in tongues and they prophesied.' However, God is not limited by that. He can still baptise you even in your own home alone or in your car or anywhere you are right now if you ask from the bottom of your heart. Yes, you can! Jesus said in Luke 11v13 'If you then who are evil know how to give good gifts to your children, how much more will your heavenly Father give the Holy Spirit to those who ask Him?' Do I need to say anything more at all? It is all very clear what you have to do.

What do you reckon? Do you think you are ready for this? Let us place the order dear friend and see how alive you can be. Hold on Salome, by the way what about speaking in tongues. Will I not make a fool of myself speaking in tongues because I heard that comes in the package? Do I have to speak in tongues or I can say to the Spirit, 'I will pass on that one?'

Jesus, our Saviour the one who baptises us in the Spirit said this about those who believe in Him, Mark 16v17 'And these signs shall follow those who believe, in My name, they shall cast out demons ----they shall speak in new tongues---.' On the day of Pentecost they all spoke in new tongues. In Acts 19 from verse 6, it says that when Paul laid his hands on those Ephesians, they all spoke in tongues. In 1 Corinthians 12 Paul goes out of his way to explain all the gifts of the Spirit and in verse 10 he mentioned the gift of tongues. Well, the gift comes with the package. Praying in tongues is so refreshing and guess what? The devil does not understand that language, so there is something to be excited about. It is a language that only God can understand, how good is that? When you speak in tongues you edify yourself. You build your spiritual muscles when you pray in tongues. You are in the spiritual gym building your muscles, ready to tackle whatever comes your way in the name of Jesus. I Corinthians 14v4, 'He who speaks in a tongue edifies himself'. When you pray in the Spirit you start to hear from God. Your spiritual ears are in tune with the Spirit of God.

I like watching Better Homes and Gardens on TV on Fridays and the part I like best is when they renovate a kitchen, bathroom or when they reconstruct a backyard. They show you the backyard or kitchen before it is renovated and then they show you what they have to do to make the

No Second Thoughts About This One — Ask For The Holy Spirit

changes. They make it look so easy but we all know that reconstructing a backyard is not an easy job. Anyway, the breathtaking moment that I love to see comes when they keep showing pictures of before and after. This is when I sit at the edge of my seat and go wow! It is hard to believe that a once run down backyard with dry weeds and a crunchy lawn can have life in less than two days. It is amazing what can be done to a lifeless garden when someone puts their effort into it.

That is what happens in our dry and run down lives when the Holy Spirit works in us. At the end, everyone goes Wow when they see the before and after in our lives.

Peter the apostle, promised Jesus that he would die with and for Him, Luke 22 v33. He just knew what to say that fellow and he never ran out of ideas. One day he wanted to build tents for Jesus, Moses and Elijah at the Mount of transfiguration and the bible actually says he was that scared he did not know what he was talking about. We all say weird staff sometimes and I can so relate to the Apostle Peter. We all have courage until we are faced with death, especially death of the cross.

The **'courageous'** Peter denied Jesus three times the same night he had promised that he would die for Him. I am not judging Peter here. I would have denied Him maybe ten times who knows, but I want you to picture the scared man denying his master for fear of the Jews. Jesus was not surprised at all! He had already told Peter that He would deny him anyway. Maybe Peter was brave enough to follow the crowds because the other disciples had already done a runner. They were all scared; they used to live in locked rooms for fear of the Jews, especially after Jesus was crucified. Peter and the rest of the Apostles had lost hope; Peter went back to fishing with the rest of the crew because nothing made sense without Jesus being around anymore. They were scared and hopeless. That was Peter and the rest of the apostles before the day of Pentecost.

Now let us look at Peter after the day of Pentecost! Wow! He was the key note speaker and apparently three thousand people gave their lives to Christ after his first sermon. Wow! Look at Peter before and after Pentecost. What a change! Did you know that all the apostles got the title 'men who turn cities upside down?' Acts 17 v 6b! Can you believe that they chose to die instead of denying Christ as their risen Lord and Saviour? It is amazing what the Holy Spirit can do to a bunch of scared and confused men if He fills them up.

For people to take up even the simplest job like waiting at the tables, they had to be filled with the Holy Spirit; Acts 6. This is how much the early church valued the power of the Holy Spirit. Nothing was done without first talking to the Spirit and the Spirit told them what to do. It was awesome. They were led by the Spirit and they worked with the Spirit. The acts of the Apostles were actually the acts of The Holy Spirit!

There are gifts that come to us when we receive the Holy Spirit.

1 Corinthians 12 (NKJV)

Spiritual Gifts: Unity in Diversity

12 "Now concerning spiritual *gifts,* brethren, I do not want you to be ignorant: ² You know that you were Gentiles, carried away to these dumb idols, however you were led. ³ Therefore I make known to you that no one speaking by the Spirit of God calls Jesus accursed, and no one can say that Jesus is Lord except by the Holy Spirit.

⁴ There are diversities of gifts, but the same Spirit. ⁵ There are differences of ministries, but the same Lord. ⁶ And there are diversities of activities, but it is the same God who works all in all. ⁷ But the manifestation of the Spirit is given to each one for the profit *of all:* ⁸ for to one is given the word of wisdom through the Spirit, to another the word of knowledge through the same Spirit, ⁹ to another faith by the same Spirit, to another gifts of healings by the same[b] Spirit, ¹⁰ to another the working of miracles, to another prophecy, to another discerning of spirits, to another *different* kinds of tongues, to another the interpretation of tongues. ¹¹ But one and the same Spirit works all these things, distributing to each one individually as He wills."

Need I say more? We do not cherry-pick the gifts we want and throw away the ones we do not like. The Spirit Himself gives us these gifts for the glory of God and the work in His Kingdom. Every citizen of the Kingdom of God must be filled with the Holy Spirit so we can do the work that Christ asked us to do.

Jesus told His disciples that it was to our advantage that He would go away so that the Helper could come. John 16 v5-11 says "But now I go away to Him who sent Me, and none of you asks Me, 'Where are You going?' ⁶ But because I have said these things to you, sorrow has filled your heart. ⁷ Nevertheless I tell you the truth. It is to your advantage that I go away; for if I do not go away, the Helper will not come to you; but if I depart, I will send Him to you. ⁸ And when He has come, He will convict the world of sin, and of righteousness, and of judgment: ⁹ of sin, because they do not believe in Me; ¹⁰ of righteousness, because I go to My Father and you see Me no more; ¹¹ of judgment, because the ruler of this world is judged."

Jesus told His disciples that it was good that he had to go to heaven so the Holy Spirit could come. There was no way in the world we were going to do God's work without the Holy Spirit. The work of the Father is done by the Spirit of the Father. Jesus commissioned us to go out into the world and preach the good news of the Kingdom of God. He told us that we would do the works that He did and even greater! He told His disciples to wait in Jerusalem before they could start any ministry. Why? Because they had to wait for the Holy Spirit to come.

Acts 1 v 4-8 says, ⁴ "And being assembled together with *them,* He commanded them not to depart from Jerusalem, but to wait for the Promise of the Father, which," *He said,* "you have heard from Me; ⁵ for John truly baptized with water, but you shall be baptized with the Holy Spirit not many days from now." ⁶ Therefore, when they had come together, they asked Him, saying, "Lord, will You at this time restore the kingdom to Israel?" ⁷ And He said to them, "It is not for you to know times or seasons which the Father has put in His own authority. ⁸ But you shall receive power when the Holy Spirit has come upon you; and you shall be witnesses to Me in Jerusalem, and in all Judea and Samaria, and to the end of the earth."

"Then you shall receive power," Jesus said. We cannot do anything in life without the power of the Holy Spirit. Jesus Himself had to be filled with the Holy Spirit too to start His ministry. The bible says on the day Jesus was baptised, the heavens opened and the Spirit descended upon Him in the form of a dove. The Spirit led Jesus into the wilderness to pray and be tempted by the devil.

Jesus always leads us by example. If He had to wait for the Holy Spirit to start His ministry, who are we to think we can do life without the Spirit of God?

Will you pray with me?

Lord Jesus you are the baptiser. You are the one who baptises me with your Spirit if I ask and I ask now that you fill me with your Holy Spirit. Forgive me of my sins and Jesus I welcome you in my life as my Lord. I surrender all to you now. Holy Spirit, I honour you as God, please come and overshadow me and refresh my life. I pray this prayer in the name of Jesus. Amen.

Do not worry if you do not feel anything at all. Start thanking God for His Holy Spirit. You will not regret this experience and that is all I can say.

Your prayer life will definitely change. You will understand the Word of God more because the Holy Spirit is the author of the bible and He will lead you into all truth. You will feel love for the saints and for everyone like you never felt before. You will have peace that the world cannot give. You are guaranteed self-control. The Spirit will give you faith to do the will of the Father.

CHAPTER 6

Provision Is On The Menu So Let Us Place Our Order

God provides for our needs. Yes He does, no arguing about that one. This is an area where if we do not get the kingdom principles right, you would think that Christians are materialistic and they are commercialising their faith. Well, it is on God's menu to provide for His children just like any earthly father would. Sometimes He just spoils us like any generous dad would. That is so biblical so do not ever feel bad going before God to ask for things because Jesus actually commanded us to ask.

Matthew 7v7 says, 'Ask, and it will be given to you; seek, and you will find; knock, and it will be opened to you. [8] For everyone who asks receives, and he who seeks finds, and to him who knocks it will be opened. [9] Or what man is there among you who, if his son asks for bread, will give him a stone? [10] Or if he asks for a fish, will he give him a serpent? [11] If you then, being evil, know how to give good gifts to your children, how much more will your Father who is in heaven give good things to those who ask Him!'

We should ask to receive, knock for the door to be opened and seek to find. Why would Jesus tell you and I to ask if that was not a proper thing to do? In John 14v14 Jesus said "If you ask anything in my name

I will do it." Well, call that bragging if you like, but we are called to do what our master asked us to do.

One thing we have to remember is that for God to provide for us, we have to belong to the Kingdom as His children. John 1 v 12 says that to those who have believed in His son God gave them power to become children of God. We become God's children the moment we believe in our hearts that Jesus is the son of God and that He died for our sins. If we confess with our mouths what we believe, then we become children of God.

This is not segregation. It is only fair. You do not get paid by Qantas if you do not work for them and signed a contract that you are one of them. Those discounts Air Zimbabwe staff get, are only for their own staff not for all of us to enjoy. In short, what I am saying is that you have to belong to a company for them to pay you. It is only fair isn't it?

Here is His deal, just believe in His Son and you can start claiming all the benefits. This is the easiest deal I have ever heard of in my life; to believe in Jesus and that is it, I am in and I can start flicking through the bible asking for the things that are promised to me. This is not a "get saved and get things" message. We are in a relationship, not a contract.

I like what Paul says in Philippians 4 v 19,

'Our God shall supply all our needs according to His riches in glory by Christ Jesus.' What makes me smile when I read this verse is that God supplies my needs according to His riches, not mine! The bible does not say according to my pay cheque, otherwise that would be sad for some of us if our pay cheques were not that hefty.

What restaurant would risk its reputation by putting something on their menu that they cannot provide? I have never worked in a restaurant or owned one but my assumption is that workers and the owner sit down first to discuss what they can put on the menu, depending on what the chefs can cook. The owner cannot insist on putting a very complicated meal that no one can cook just because it looks nice on the menu. All I am saying is, the owner, if he cannot cook must see what his or her chefs

Provision Is On The Menu So Let Us Place Our Order

can cook then add that on the menu. If there is no one to make a quiche then the owner should not add that on their list.

Why would God the creator of the heavens and earth, risk His reputation by saying He will provide the desires of our hearts or our needs if He could not do it? Jesus even confirmed this when He asked the question what father would give their son a snake if they asked for a fish? He then goes on to say if we who are evil know how to give good things to our children, how much will our Father in heaven give good things to those who ask? Jesus is saying our Father will provide for us for His name's sake.

People brag and lie sometimes or change their minds after making a promise but our God is not like you and I. I have promised my kids a trip to Disney Land but for reasons best known to me and my husband, we have not gone yet or I do not know if we will at all. In short, we cannot do that yet because we have got fees to pay and mortgages. See I can change my mind and it is legal, but the bible says in Numbers 23v19 'God is not man that He should lie nor is He a son of man that He should change His mind. Will He not say and will He not do?' Look, God is the only One who has made Himself servant of His own word. In fact the bible says that God has exalted His word high above His name, Psalm 138v2 confirms that. Let us say God is a Man of His word in modern terminology. He is like a manufacturer who makes sure His products are of good reputation because He knows His name is on the line.

Right! So you reckon you can order provision from the menu? It is there for sure and the owner of the restaurant would not put it there if it could not be cooked at the back. I have done this since the moment I realised who I am and what was entitled to me as a child of a King. Where can I start? I am one of the people who sing the song, 'What the Lord has done for me I cannot tell it all'. I would want you to read this and know that I am not exaggerating to make God look big; He is already big, so I am telling you my friend one testimony after another and it is all very true for the glory of our God.

We came to Australia in 2001 with suitcases on our backs and our three kids aged 2, 6 and 10. My husband was studying at one of the universities in Perth. I thought that me being a teacher, all I needed to do was to go to the Education Department in Perth and present my qualifications and well, I would be teaching in no time. No, things do not happen that way to overseas trained teachers. Your qualifications have to be assessed first and that takes weeks and weeks, so I was without a job for a while. We decided to look for cleaning jobs and we were surprised to learn that they needed resumes for that too. It was not that easy even to get a cleaning job. We finally got a cleaning job where both my husband and I worked as a team. This was months after we had arrived in Australia so by now, all of our savings from Zimbabwe were all gone to rent and food of course. Our rent had now started falling behind and food was really scarce. Our phone was disconnected because we had missed a few payments. We were starting to panic. We hardly knew anyone in Perth at that stage.

So one day we only had left over food from the previous night and that is what I packed in the kids' lunch boxes and I left a small amount for my husband and I. The plan was to have a breakfast of the leftover food around eleven in the morning, that way we would have lunch covered too. I knew we needed to get money from somewhere to buy food, but I had no idea where from exactly. So I had a wonderful suggestion to make to my husband. I asked him if he could go and borrow some money, about ten dollars from the two Zimbabwean students we had met once, near where we lived and give the money back the same week after we got paid. So Fidelis agreed to do that and he went to see the two boys from Zimbabwe. The boys were that happy to see Fidelis and before he could explain why he was visiting them they said to him, 'Mr Chifamba we are so glad that you are here. We have not had food for two days and we are starving, would it be possible to come to your house and eat?' Most students or families coming from Zimbabwe at the time were having difficulty getting money sent from home due to the critical foreign currency problems the country was experiencing. My husband did not even hesitate, 'Of course you can, we have food at our house". There is a fine line between craziness and faith!

So after a couple of minutes my husband turned up on our door step with two hungry boys and he explained to me that they needed food, which I confirmed we had. So I served the last meal we had in the house. 'Oh Mrs Chifamba you don't know what you have done' said the boys. 'You don't know what you have done either boys', I thought to myself with a smile on my face and tears welling in my eyes. The boys left. I went into my bedroom and I started to cry and laugh at the same time. 'Lord you have got a very high sense of humour. I told you that I needed food in the house and to answer my prayer you sent two boys who are hungry here, what's going on?" I had a good talk with God and asked Him if He had really understood my prayer. I was in need, not in a position to give.

Did I say our God supplies our needs? Yes I did and He did it for us. The following morning I went to drop off the kids at school (by the way a Zambian friend of ours whom we had only met once too, had lent us $10.00 the day we had the drama, so we had food for the kids for school). So I was coming back from my children's school and as I got to my door step, I saw bags of food just resting on the fly screen. I thought I was lost so I double checked to see if I was at the right address and sure enough it was my place. I could not believe my eyes. These things do not happen every day you know! On top of one of the bags was a note, 'Salome, Father P had asked me to take this food to a home of these elderly nuns but when I got there, the place was closed. So I decided to take the food to your house before I even talked to Father P. I saw you at church once with little kids so I thought of you when I found out the place was closed. My name is M". Coincidence? Definitely not! That is what I call providence. Since that day, Father P told this wonderful lady to bring the food to our house. So every Wednesday we enjoyed the food and we used to call it 'manna'. So we had 'manna' for quite some time until we had proper jobs, then it stopped coming because Father P had found another family who needed help. How timely was that?

We also worked for a company that looks after people with disabilities in their own homes. We loved our jobs as carers and enjoyed the work. After working for some time, we decided to buy a decent car and we got a Daihatsu Terios. I was that proud of that car but we needed money to pay it off. So here we were praying to God for more shifts so we could pay off our car sooner than five years. One day at work I heard that the company was making some structural changes and they were going to end up with two vacant houses which needed house keepers. The house keepers were to live in the houses for three months, for free and only pay for their bills. So we put our hands up for one of the houses and a good friend must have recommended us. Core workers tried to reason with us that three months of free rent was not worth moving the whole family for. We were willing to take the chance and we did.

Before we knew it we were living in a four bed roomed house, fully furnished in one of the good suburbs in Perth, Willetton, for free. How good is that? We lived in that house for more than 18 months and we left the house when we moved to South Australia. Other employees of the same company tried to apply for the same house after we left, but they were told that the houses were soon to be used for respite so no one could live in them after we left. I do not know about you, but I do not take these things lightly. Someone used to come and mow the lawn for us while we were in that house. Windows were cleaned for us while we were there. I had to get used to that. We had never had that happen to us before.

We did not even struggle paying for our car, in fact my husband wanted a Honda CRV so we went hunting for one.

If you are working and earning reasonably good money, do you still have to ask for God's help? Most certainly yes! We need God's help and provision every day. Well isn't that being greedy? Of course not, you are just being a child of a loving Father who wants to be involved in every part of your life. To cut a long story short we went hunting for the Honda but the car yards we visited did not have Hondas. We nearly bought a Nissan Extrail because we were tired of looking. The next day we wanted to go and finalise the Nissan deal but we thought once more we would have another look somewhere else, to see if we could not find a good second hand Honda CRV. We stopped at one of the car yards and we started looking. This salesperson came to us and started asking us if we wanted a car. Before we even told him the sort we were looking for, the sales person asked if we had ever tried a Honda CRV. I tell you my husband and I looked at each other and went, 'Yes'. We were that surprised we just went in, saw the car and bought it. Do not settle for second best. God will give you the desires of your heart.

I do not know why but for some reason I thought being poor is biblical and that is what God meant by being humble, until I read the stories of Abraham, Isaac, Jacob, Solomon etc. Boy, those men were that rich. It is recorded in the bible and yet they were humble before God (they were not perfect of course but that's what gives me hope. The bible does not white wash its characters).

So our God is a God of provision and He loves to prosper His kids, just like any devoted dad would. In fact, David in Psalms 37v25 says that since he had been young he had never seen a child of God begging for bread nor the righteous forsaken. This does not mean that Christians live a cushy life and never have financial problems. We all do have our fair share of problems but our God gives us breakthroughs and provision.

So do we need to go to work then? Yes, please go to work. God does not bless the lazy but the work of our hands. Check Deuteronomy 28v14 onwards. There! What do you think of that? One blessing after another! Let us check the scriptures shall we? If my eyes are not playing tricks with me, God said in that chapter, 'if you obey His voice ----"then the blessings will overtake us." We play a part in this.

We must do life according to God's word then the blessings will be added to us. God's word is meant to prosper us and protect us. It is meant for our own good. Therefore reading His word, and praying to God for the grace to live according to His word will align us with His blessings. Fair enough! What dad would give his credit card to a child who is not honest? If you steal money in the house all the time and instead of paying bills, you buy drugs, you cannot blame your parents if they do not trust you with their money. So God is not asking us to be perfect so we could be blessed, but just obeying His word then the blessing will come. That's not a big ask is it?

When I first got saved, I did not like to hear the word tithe. I associated that with churches who wanted to take my money. I did not know that tithing was for me, not for the Pastor. In Malachi 3v10 God promised to protect my money from the devourer. That is for my own benefit, not for the church. I actually do not care what the church does with my tithe, I just want the windows of heaven to open and for God to pour out a big blessing, too much for me to receive it. If there are Pastors out there abusing God's money, that is their problem, they are answerable to God. My part is to obey His word, pay my tithe and see what God has in store for me. So tithing is one of those things we as Christians are expected to do and we do not need to see if the Pastor has got a new pair of shoes and wondering if that was not my tithe from last week. Try tithing my friend, it is the only thing God Himself asked you to try Him with and I can assure you windows of heaven will open.

In 2005 we moved to Port Pirie in South Australia and we rented a house, for about a year. In 2006 we decided to buy a house so we prayed about it. One day I drove along a street called Arthur Street just having a look and I saw a "For Sale" sign on one of the houses. I fell in love with the house so I went home and told my husband and kids and we all went and had a look from outside. We agreed we wanted the house so we made an appointment with the Real Estate Agent and we went through the house. We all agreed it was what we wanted so we made an offer. I went to work the following day (I was doing relief teaching) and as I cleaned up the desk for the teacher I was relieving, I saw a piece of paper advertising for home loans for teachers. I wrote down the number on a piece of paper and rang the loan people that evening. I was assigned to a loan broker who was very keen to help me.

'Salome do you work full time or part time?' he asked and I told him that I was only casual or a relief teacher. 'What about your husband is he full time or part time?' and again I told him that my husband was also a casual worker. 'This is going to be interesting', he said. Anyway, the guy took all our details and said he would get back to me. Later on during the week, the gentleman rang me and told me that none of the banks were willing to give us a 100% loan since we were not Australian residents yet, so we had to raise a deposit of 20%. Well 20% of the offer we had made on the house was coming to $30,000 which is a lot of money and we did not have that kind of money. The broker wanted to know if we were able to raise $30,000 and I told him we could. Let me make it clear to you all my friends, we did not have that kind of money and we could not raise that much. We only had less than $500 in the bank. I did not want to tell the broker that we were going to pray about it because I knew he would hang up on me if he was not a Christian.

So we prayed about it with friends and I asked a friend of mine in Perth to join me in prayer. My friend in Perth told me that this was strange that I asked her to pray about it because she had just sold her house and wanted to deposit for another house but God had told her to wait. Well believe it or not the next day after we prayed my friend rang me and told me that they were going to lend us the $30,000. She said she knew God was in this because her husband did not even think twice about it when she asked him about lending us $30,000. (He could not be bothered since he was watching a game of footy. He said yes without any hesitations). Who does not stop and think seriously about thirty thousand dollars because they are watching footy? Is footy really that important? That can only be God.

So I rang the broker and told him that we had raised $30,000 so he went back to the bank with the news. Well, since we were not residents of Australia yet, the broker said we could not qualify for the government first home owner's grant so we had to raise another $7,500 on top of the $30,000. My heart sank but again, I told the broker that I was going to raise the amount. So we prayed. That same week our tax returns came back and we received some money but we were still a few thousand dollars short to raise the $7,500. That same week I got a letter from the Education Department to say that they had reviewed my salary and back dated it because they were underpaying me. They were paying me as a junior teacher while they waited for evidence from the Education Department in Zimbabwe that I had taught there for 10 years. So I got backdated and the money was enough to raise the $7,500.

The broker let the bank know that we had enough money for the deposit. The bank, however, discovered that we had a default on our credit record and the broker told us that that was the end of the story. I was not even aware that we had a default and we were told it stays on our records for 5 years. I was so disappointed and I asked who had given us the default. I told the broker that I had evidence of all the payments I had made and how we had made new arrangements to make payments to this particular company when we moved from Perth to Adelaide. We put all the evidence together but still the broker was convinced that this particular bank would not give us the loan because of the credit record. He said he was willing to try which he did and ...we got the loan!!! I remember the broker saying, "I don't know why the bank gave you this loan." Well I know why, Jesus said in Matthew 21v22 "Whatever things you ask for in prayer believing you will receive."

He is faithful to His word and we are living proof. With no money to talk about in the bank, no full time or part time jobs, no permanent residence in Australia and with a default on our credit record, God still gave us a house. This is what I would call against all odds; God gave us a house according to His riches in glory by Christ Jesus.

Coming to Australia was a big deal for us. This meant leaving all that we knew and our families. We were not sure at first if God was in the whole idea. I was that scared I had to ask God to confirm it all. One day I said to God, 'if this going to Australia thing is Your idea, please let someone who does not know about this ask me about it, then I will know You are in this." I had to do this since I was not that keen initially to leave my family. I went to work that day and just before we started, this lady at work who was a very nice person, but not that close to me at all since we worked different sessions, came to me and said, "Salome are you praying for something?" I just stared at her for some seconds and I asked her why she wanted to know. She said "I don't know Salome but I had a dream and God asked me to ask you if you are praying for something." Well I do not call that coincidence my friend because that was all I needed to hear from God and we packed to come.

The only problem was we had to pay part of my husband's school fees to get the student visa and we also needed money for airfares and other expenses to settle in Australia. I can remember our son pacing the floor praying for the money to go to Australia (he was only ten then). It was hard at that time to get foreign currency in Zimbabwe from the banks and there were huge waiting lists to get money. We did not know how we were going to get the money to pay my husband's fees so we prayed. An amazing thing happened. My husband's boss, where he worked in Zimbabwe, rang him at home to see if he could delay his plans to Australia by a few weeks. Another miracle was that my husband had been granted study leave, much to our amazement and to the glory of God. That meant that he would continue to receive his salary while away. Fidelis asked why and he was told that the lady who was going to Indonesia, Thailand and Malaysia with the Minister of Tourism and Industry delegation had fallen sick and could not go so the boss wanted to know if Fidelis could go on that trip. By the way Fidelis had taken two weeks annual leave prior to his study leave so the boss could have picked someone else. Fidelis went on that trip and all his daily allowances and other allowances he saved from that trip were enough to cover all our expenses. What do we call that? God's providence. It is there on the menu. Go ahead and order it please.

Many men of God in the bible, who were well known, were very rich. So does the bible say. Abraham had a lot of wealth and there was a time when he and his nephew Lot, had to split up because they had a lot of animals and the grazing land was not big enough. Isaac, the bible said, became prosperous as God blessed him (check Genesis 26v13-14). Jacob prospered when he worked for his uncle Laban and Laban himself noticed it (Genesis 30v27). Laban told his nephew Jacob that he had learnt from experience that he was being blessed because of Jacob. Esau was a blessed man too. Talk of Joseph the son of Jacob! He was not only rich, but was the most important man in Egypt after Pharaoh. God raises his own, from the dungeon to the palace.

Let us get this right, we do not become Christians to be rich. We become Christians so we can have a relationship with God, then God blesses us as He sees fit. It is a process we go through as Christians. God knows when we are mature enough to handle a lot of money. He knows that sometimes money can take our focus from Him, so He prepares us through a process. We do that with our kids. I never gave my kids thousands of dollars for pocket money when they were little. I do not do that even now that they are older! I gave them pocket money according to their needs and their level of maturity. Our little girl would have spent all her money on toys and lollies. That is what she dreamt of when she was little. So we knew not to give her too much pocket money for the simple reason that she would have spent it all on lollies.

We moved from Perth to Adelaide with very little money. The move was part of the condition for us to get a permanent visa in Australia. A friend of mine in Roxby Downs offered to look after the kids for us while we looked for a house to rent in Adelaide. We had not told our friends that we did not have any money at all for rent or food. My friend's friend who is now one of my best friends, offered to look after us while we looked for a house in Adelaide. Let me make this clear, this lady who offered us her house and food did not know us that well. God used that lady to look after us and then friends lent us some money for rent and food because it took a while for us to get jobs in Adelaide. These friends of ours did not complain about the delay on our part to give them back their money. I do not encourage anyone to take such risks with kids but we did not have that much of a choice. What if my friend was not willing to help with the kids? What if that lady did not want to help? All I am saying is God puts people in our paths to provide for us and we are forever grateful to God for providing good friends in our lives.

Having said that and having shared that, do you think you could ask God to provide for you now? All you have to do is ask. How does that sound?

CHAPTER 7

ORDER GUIDANCE; IT IS THERE ON THE MENU

A very old fairy tale talks of a girl who got lost, then went to ask for directions from a certain man. "Sir I am lost and I do not know which route to take." The man asked the little girl, "where have you come from and where are you going?" The little girl replied "I do not know where I have come from and I don't know where I am going." So the man replied "take any route then if you don't know where you have come from and where you are going. Any route will take you anywhere."

The bible actually says that people without a vision perish. If we do not know what we want in life or not sure of where we have come from, then anything goes. That is a very unhealthy way of living. Sometimes we can relate to the little girl in the story because we do not know where we are going.

Have you ever felt like you have come to the cross roads of life and you do not know what to do or what decision to make? I have felt like that so many times, so join the club. It is very normal to run out of ideas on what to do or to be unsure on what decision to make regarding an issue. God has given us a free will to make our own decisions in life, good or bad. God never forces us into anything but if we ask Him, He is very happy to make the best decisions in our lives. Let me put it this way, God is willing to guide us. The bible says, "the steps of a righteous man are ordered by the Lord." Psalms 37v23. He leads us when we ask.

So are you having problems on what decision to make on a certain issue? Nothing makes sense and you do not know what to do? Scroll down while you are still looking at the menu. There! Guidance is on the menu so it is in the kitchen.

I admire a fellow called Gideon in the book of Judges in the old testament. He heard God tell him to go and attack the Midianites, who were harassing the children of Israel year after year. Before Gideon could do as he was told, he asked God to confirm it three times so he could be sure it was God who had asked him to do that task (Judges 6 v1-27). Sometimes we are faced with a big task to do and we feel God has asked us to do it, but we still want God to confirm it. That is not a sin, it is just wanting to be sure without a shred of doubt that God is in it. Someone said you cannot serve God with a question mark on your head. How so true that is. Sometimes an idea sounds good and you think this is the thing to do but we still need to ask God if that is in His will.

I remember when one day I was just complaining to God on why He had brought us to Port Pirie. I said to Him, 'Why God did you bring us to Port Pirie? We cannot get jobs and we don't seem to be helping any one at all?' I was quite upset that day and I was so sure God had brought us to Port Pirie but I could not work out why. My husband did not have a proper job yet, so he was just doing casual work here and there. I was doing relief teaching and that was not reliable either. We both had applied for I don't know how many jobs with no success. I was not sure we were of any help anywhere and I was starting to question the decision to move to Pirie from Adelaide.

Anyway, I went to a nursery shop in Pirie just to have a look at some plants and there I met a friend of ours. I said hello and asked how his wife was and before I could say bye this friend said, from nowhere, "Salome don't you ever think you are not doing anything in Pirie. Those healing services we are doing are a big breakthrough. Nothing like that has ever

Order Guidance; It Is There On The Menu

happened here," I just stood there staring at our friend. I could not believe it. I thought just five minutes before, I was whinging about if we were in the right place or not and there God used someone to answer that for me. I think God spoke to me that day and I never doubted again if it was His will to be in Pirie. Well, we love Port Pirie and we do not question the decision to move there any more.

Our God is a speaking God. He has a mouth and if we ask Him for directions, He tells us exactly where to go and how. Are you at the cross roads of a big decision? Are you worried about making the wrong decision about something and you do not know who to ask for help? Let me say this dear friend, knock for God's help and He will open the door for you.

Our son has always wanted to be a pilot and we thought it was just a childhood fantasy that would go away one day, but surprisingly he sounded serious about it up to high school. We lived in Perth when we first arrived in Australia and there were only two schools, if not one, who offer aviation as a subject in high school. So when we heard about one of the schools we thought that our son would apply to go there for high school. We were that excited but we did not know that one had to sit for an exam to get a place there.

Anyway, our son was keen to write the exam so we registered him for it. I was a bit relaxed because I did not think that a lot of kids would be interested in that subject, so I was shocked when we arrived for the exam to see a room packed with kids, about 200 or more. I expressed my surprise and as if to put me off, one of the parents commented that another group of kids, probably more than this one, had sat for the same exam the previous day. That just made me so nervous, I started rehearsing what I would say to my son when the results came out. What really made me worry was the fact that they only wanted 32 kids for that course.

After the exam, we asked our son how he had gone in the exam and all we got was "pretty good." Trust me, that is a long answer from our boy. Anyway, the results came and our son was among the 37 they had picked, but he was one of the five on the waiting list. I thought that my son would be disappointed but no, he just said all would be well. A few months later, I thought I would ring the school to hear what was going on with the aviation class. The receptionist told me that they had already done the enrolment process and there were no chances at all of another child being enrolled. They had even done the orientation, the receptionist told me.

Well, that did not stop me from asking if I could talk to the teacher in charge of that subject and the receptionist was polite enough to put me through. The teacher in charge explained everything, just as the receptionist had explained and said they would let me know if anything changed. Let me say this to someone. It is never over until God says it is over. The following day, that teacher rang me to say one of the students had just moved interstate with his parents and they were offering my boy a place for aviation. I screamed on the phone and I am glad that teacher did not think I was a nut case because he did not hang up on me.

The steps of a righteous man are guided by the Lord. I believe that, otherwise we would not be where we are today. When we came to Port Pirie, we thought that our son's desire to be a pilot would be gone, since there was nothing really to be an incentive at that time. Did I say that God is not limited by our little minds? Yes of course He is not. It wasn't long after we arrived in Pirie when we heard that one of the private schools was offering an aviation programme. We thanked God, our son was accepted in the programme and that kept him focused on his dream. Let me just say this, as parents we were not very sure if our son could pull the grades he needed. So the results came out for our son in December, while we were on holiday in Queensland with the kids. My son was 12 points short of the required points to get into his Aviation course at the University he had applied for.

We were heartbroken and while we were trying to get to terms with that, friends were ringing to find out how our son had gone. I tell you, sometimes you feel like lying but that does not help in any way. The truth always comes out anyway! It was painful and embarrassing for us, but our son seemed oblivious to all that. He was having the best time on the rides and he even came to us and said, "Mum and Dad thank you so much this is the best holiday of my life!" Really son? I do not know if he knew the implications of his results.

Anyway, we went back home after the holiday. A few days later I heard my son shouting, "Mum I made it in" and I thought maybe he was playing a game or something. He had his hand in the air waving in joy, so I asked what he meant and he said, "Mum I got accepted into University for my course." I nearly passed out. Well, let us cut the long story short. My son got into University to do aviation. The steps of a righteous man are ordered by the Lord indeed. Later on, a friend asked how my son got in with the points he had and my answer was, "only God knows."

So are you still not sure of what to do? Pray my friend, God is listening even to the smallest thing concerning your life. He said it in Matthew 7v7, "seek and you will find." Seek His direction and you will find a way and trust me, God knows our needs better than we do.

Coming to Australia was a big deal, like I have already mentioned. When my husband suggested that we move to Australia, I was the first one to say no and I did not want him to suggest that again! I thought I had it all. Who wouldn't? I had a three-bedroomed apartment and a job and I was very happy to commute every day to work using public transport (I had no license) and none of that bothered me. The only problem I had was that my kids were not in the best schools, nothing wrong with where they were, but I wanted more for my kids. So going overseas could have been the answer to that problem, but I did not see that as necessary. Anyway, God made a way for us to Australia.

We arrived in Australia in 2001 in August. My idea was that we would work hard and buy a big house in Zimbabwe, then go back home to our families. However, six months into our stay in Australia, I started thinking of staying in Australia for good. I did not want to go back home, so I started trying to convince my husband and kids that we should stay in

Australia for good. The kids were the first ones to say yes and my husband was quite amused that the person who did not want to leave Zimbabwe in the first place, was no longer keen to go back.

So yes, we decided to apply for a permanent visa. It takes about a year for the whole process but that did not put us off. We went ahead and applied for our permanent visa. The response came saying that we had not qualified for the visa because we did not have enough points. We were short by five points. The letter also stated that our application was going to be put in a pool and if anything changed, then the Department of Immigration would let us know. In other words, we were waiting for 'an angel to come and stir up the water in the pool' because not much happens in those pools. We were very distraught but we continued to pray for the visa even though our faith was really low.

> Dear Ms Chifamba
>
> **DECISION ON VISA APPLICATION**
>
> I refer to your application for a Skilled - Independent (BN), subclass 136 Skilled - Independent visa, received in this office on 27/01/2004. I have assessed your application against the criteria for this class of visa.
>
> Attached is the decision record. This decision covers you and the following persons included in your application:
>
> CHIFAMBA, Fidelis
> CHIFAMBA, Kudzah
> CHIFAMBA, Rumbidzai
> CHIFAMBA, Rutendo
>
> To be granted a Skilled - Independent (BN), 136 Skilled - Independent visa, an applicant must achieve the pass mark when assessed against the General Points Test.
>
> You have not achieved the award of points equal to, or greater than, the applicable pass mark. However, your score does meet the applicable pool mark. This means that your application will be kept in a pool of applications. New pass marks and pool marks are set periodically. All applications in the pool will be assessed against any new pass mark or pool mark that is announced.
>
> If your score equals or exceeds a new pass mark, your application will be removed from the pool and you will be asked to satisfy any outstanding requirements.
>
> If your score falls below a new pool mark, your application will be refused.

One day a friend of ours from Zambia passed by our house to visit. He asked us how far we had gone with our visa application and reluctantly we told him that we were unsuccessful. Our friend said something profound that has stayed with us over all these years. His words were, "Don't worry my brother, Australia will introduce a new visa just for you." Who would believe that? A country will introduce a new visa just for us? Seriously? Isn't that going too far with our words and faith?

Maybe I need to tell you the story of our friend first, before I tell you what happened after he said that to us. His faith was not always that strong or profound. Two years before that, he had been studying at one of the universities in Perth in Western Australia. He lived in Perth with his wife and two kids. He started struggling to pay fees for himself and for the kids too. He tried to work hard to meet his needs but unfortunately he could not. He got a letter to say that he had to take the family back to Zambia and then come back and work for his fees. The thought of taking his wife and kids back home really affected him badly. So he came to our house one day to tell us about his problem. Unfortunately, my husband was not home so he did not even bother to sit down. He just started talking about his problem. He was pacing up and down the lounge area and I could tell he was very upset. I rang my husband who was at university on that day, to talk to him. My husband rang him and he started again telling my husband his problem. Our friend was very anxious and upset, even on the phone. All I heard later on was "Amen, Amen," several times which meant they were praying for a solution. After that he sounded calmer and he left with his two little kids. They could not work out why their Dad was that upset on that particular day.

Praise be to our God, a few weeks later our friend came to see us, this time beaming from ear to ear. God had answered his prayers in a miraculous way. The church he attended had heard about his predicament, so they all offered to pay for his fees and his children's fees. They did not pay his fees for that semester only, but for his entire duration of study which was three years. The church also paid his bills and rent. The man and his wife were over the moon. Their faith grew in less than six months to unbelievable heights. So no wonder he had the faith to tell us that God was going to introduce a new visa for us. But when you are in a very difficult situation, sometimes your faith really goes down and it can be hard to believe the promises of God on our lives.

Our friend said that Australia would introduce a new visa just for us in April and sure enough, we got a letter in July and here is what it said; "Australia has introduced a new visa called Skilled Independent regional Visa" or SIR in short. The letter then stated that we had enough points to qualify for the visa and we could go ahead and nominate a state that would sponsor us for the visa. We then nominated South Australia and that is how we ended up in South Australia from Perth, in Western Australia. I keep records of these things because they sound so out of this world and I think people even question our sanity sometimes when we tell these testimonies.

> Salome Chifamba
> 22 Helsall Court
> Willetton
> WA
> 6155
>
> Dear Salome Chifamba,
>
> **Invitation to apply for the Skilled – Independent Regional (SIR) (Provisional)**
>
> On 12 January 2004 the Australian Government announced the introduction of a new visa for skilled migrants who wished to live in a regional or low population growth area in Australia but were unable to meet the criteria to be granted a permanent visa. The new visa, the Skilled – Independent Regional (SIR) (Provisional) visa, will come into effect on 1 July 2004 and has been developed in consultation with State/Territory Governments.
>
> The visa has been designed to:
> - address skill shortages that may exist in regional areas; and
> - encourage a more balanced dispersal of Australia's skilled migrant intake.
>
> While SIR visa applicants are still required to pass the points test, the pass mark is slightly lower than that currently applied to Independent Skilled Migration visas. The current pass mark for the SIR visa is 110 points.
>
> A SIR (Provisional) visa will allow the holder to remain in Australia for a period of three years provided they live and work in regional Australia. As part of the application, applicants for the SIR (Provisional) visa will be required to sign an undertaking that they, and the members of their family unit, will not live, work, or study outside regional Australia or a low population metropolitan area for the duration of their SIR (Provisional) visa. A condition requiring SIR visa holders to honour these undertakings will be attached to the visa, though short absences from regional Australia will be permitted.

What is that? Coincidence? No way! That is what I call *GOD-INCEDENCES* and they only happen when we pray and believe.

Order Guidance; It Is There On The Menu

Do not despair my friend. Do not give up. When Jesus told His disciples to launch into the deep after toiling all night and catching nothing, it sounded a bit crazy; Luke 5v4-5. These men were fishermen by profession. They knew when to give up in the fishing business. Washing their nets was a sign that it was over for the day. It is never over until Jesus says it is over. Peter tried to explain how that would not work but he eventually said, "Nevertheless at your word Lord I will do it." It is like saying, it does not make sense God but I will do it anyway. And he did! What happened? We all know the story, they caught more than they could imagine. No wonder they immediately left their nets and followed Jesus. I know a few things about men, now that I have been married for more than twenty five years! You never ask a man to do something and immediately he stands up to do it. It was different for these men. The bible tells me they immediately left their nets and followed Jesus. They had seen the evidence of the arrival of the Kingdom of God. Let us ask Him for guidance if we do not know what to do. Take the step of faith if God is asking you to do something no matter how ridiculous it sounds.

Our youngest daughter finished year 12 in 2017. She was so sure she wanted to do law and we prayed about it with her. Well, the results came out and her ATAR was not enough for law for all the universities in Adelaide. She told us that she had asked God to make it so obvious which University she had to go to. We got a little bit worried that the points she had might not let her do the course she wanted, but she had such strong faith that all would go well.

Well, the word of God says He is able to do exceedingly abundantly above and beyond our imaginations. Two universities offered her the law course she wanted to do. We were over the moon. A week before that, I had told her that God had told me that she would be going to this other university for law but when the offers came, that particular university had not offered her the course. I said to her that I think I must have heard God wrong, but we were excited that the other two universities had offered her the course. Two weeks after the offers were made, our daughter got a phone call on a weekend from that university I thought God had told me she was going to, and they offered her the law course. We were excited for her. God is faithful and let us not doubt Him when He confirms things for us, even though it might look way over the top.

Being pastors of a church was never on our prayer list or our desires. The last thing I wanted in my life was to start a church. I had seen how pastors sometimes struggle leading churches and how much of their time is needed to do God's work, so my husband and I never dreamt of being pastors.

In 2010 we felt led (after a lot of prophesies from God) to move from where we were fellowshipping. We had our eyes on one of the churches we knew and we prayed for God to confirm if we could join that particular church. We already had our bags packed ready to go to that church. While we waited for God to confirm the decision we were about to make, both my husband and I felt God speaking to us to start a church in Port Pirie. We tried to brush that aside because we knew we could not do that.

So we came back home one day from Adelaide with the kids and we turned the TV on, we had the Christian channel on. All of us froze. We could not believe our ears. Here on TV was this evangelist preaching and his message was, "You have come to the end of an era and God does not want you to stop, just keep on going." Then the preacher went on to explain that if you stop doing God's work you create commotion in the Kingdom of God. We just looked at each other with the kids. Could God be speaking to us, we wondered.

The following week, we went to visit friends and we shared with them what we felt God was saying to us and the friends sort of laughed at us (the husband especially). It was on a Saturday when we visited them and the following day we decided all to go to this particular church in Adelaide. There was a visiting pastor on that day. He started his message and he said something that made us all know that God was speaking to us. He said, "When God tells you to do something, sometimes it is church folks who will tell you that you are going crazy and laugh at you." After the service, the friend who had sort of laughed the night before, looked at us and said, "I think you need to go ahead and do what God is telling you to do."

The following month, we went to a conference and in the whole conference we felt God was confirming His word to us. This particular preacher preached on the story of Nehemiah and she said that Nehemiah did not listen to distractions but continued to do what God had told him to do. After the conference, a few of our friends came to us and told us they felt God had confirmed to us what He had told us to do.

Friends, our God still speaks today, if you ask Him for direction. He never leaves us to make it on our own. He guides us all the way. So in 2010 we stared the ministry, 'Your Kingdom Come.' In the first service we had 5 people, myself, my husband and our three kids. We were not sure where the congregants would come from. The next service we had two more people join us. The following week we had an amazing thing happen. This young girl rang us and told us that she had been referred to us by her Doctor. Now that really made us excited! A referral from the hospital to church! This young girl came and gave her life to Jesus and God made way for her which she never thought would ever happen. She was reunited with her family and God took her out of the mess she was in. Her best friend got saved too.

We started to slowly grow and we eventually could not fit in the house for a service, so we looked for a place to worship. After praying about this as a church, God blessed us with a free hall that we use every Sunday and we are forever grateful to God for the venue we have at the moment. Now we are praying as a church, for a block of land to build a sanctuary for God and we know God is going to supply our needs. We have seen people's lives transformed through this ministry and we are learning every day. We are seeing spiritual growth in this ministry, which is amazing. We as the leaders are growing everyday as we learn how to do God's work.

CHAPTER 8

TIME TO GROW UP

Well, I guess in every relationship there are ups and downs and some of the downs are not funny at all. When I started going out with my husband in my teens, I never thought that one day I would have an argument with him. We seemed to get along very well and I never saw any faults in him and I do not think he knew what he was getting himself into with me. Do you know why we never argued the first six months of our relationship? We were not married yet so we were not living together yet. After April 28th 1991, I became his wife and he became my husband.

We were soon to realise that we are two different people with different backgrounds. I did not know that he does not like shopping! Shocking huh? He was not very happy with my shopping habits! Well that was not fair on me of course, or was it? He did not know that I always want things done my way (I am getting better in this area).

All I am saying is it is not all rosy in any relationship. I had to grow up and learn what my husband likes and he did the same too (the truth is we are still learning a lot about each other). That is the same with being a Christian.

Yes we ask and receive, yes God wants to bless us and of course He looks after us, but we need to grow up in our relationship with Him.

When I became a Christian, I do not know why but I developed this arrogant attitude towards non-believers. I was not aware I was doing this and I think that was one of the first things God dealt with in me. One day I went to church and this girl in a very short skirt came forward to receive communion and I remember muttering under my breath, 'Oh God what is this?' Then another lady went to receive communion after that girl and I said something like this, 'God! She thinks that uniform is enough in a relationship with You doesn't she?' I was cruising in my judgemental journey and I thought God was agreeing with me, until I heard a voice as clear as crystal, 'Salome, all these are my children too and I love them.' Ouch! That got my attention and I had to confess big time, but did I learn my lesson? Not that fast, I am sad to say.

One day we went for home group prayers where we used to live. Before we started prayer this man walked in and everyone in the group really cheered and everyone said, "Hello Uncle", "Makadii Sekuru", in my language. He then waved at everybody in a very good mood. I straight away thought the man was drunk so I started my judgemental whinging before God. I got really annoyed by the joy on this man's face and how everyone thought he was funny. Inwardly I groaned, 'how dare he comes to prayer drunk?' I really started judging this man and the following week, as if God wanted me to learn a very good lesson, the man came again for prayer. He then started sharing the word in his jovial mood and he said, "for some of us who don't drink." My goodness didn't that make me feel like a Pharisee or even worse? I was ashamed of myself and I am still learning not to do this.

Jesus made it very clear in Mathew 7 v1-5; "Judge not, that you be not judged. ² For with what judgement you judge, you will be judged; and with the measure you use, it will be measured back to you. ³ And why do you look at the speck in your brother's eye, but do not consider the plank in your own eye? ⁴ Or how can you say to your brother, 'Let me remove the speck from your eye'; and look, a plank *is* in your own eye? ⁵ Hypocrite! First remove the plank from your own eye, and then you will see clearly to remove the speck from your brother's eye."

I cannot say I am there yet in this weakness but I am aware I have that weakness and I am asking the Holy Spirit every day to help me in this area. That also is on the menu for you my friend. If you cannot cope with issues in your life, ask the Helper to help you.

One day I was praying alone in my bedroom and I saw a vision of water, coming down from heaven, more like the Victoria Falls. It was so spectacular and seemed quite refreshing to be able to stand and let that water shower on me. I walked towards the water just so I could stand under the shower to be refreshed. As I walked closer, the water moved away from me and I took a few steps towards it again but the water moved further away from me. This happened several times as I was praying and I started to question God on what was happening? I said, 'Lord how come I am not being refreshed by this water yet, I really could do with some refreshment now?' As clear as anything I heard God saying that He really wanted to refresh me, only that I was doing something wrong. I asked God what it was I was doing wrong (not that I am perfect) but I wanted to know. Gossiping, God told me, was standing in my way to be refreshed. I was quick to defend myself because I only talked to my husband about other people and never with anyone else. God explained to me that I actually gossip so much with my husband especially about my friend, whom God reminded me about. I felt so ashamed of myself because I talked about that friend of mine with my husband and I used to judge her a lot. God told me that if I stopped gossiping about my friend He would refresh me.

Just as I was having this conversation with God, a friend of ours came to say hello and as usual we prayed before she left. She then turned around and said, 'I don't know Salome but I feel that God wants me to tell you that He wants to refresh you. Can we pray about this?'

I had my mouth open for a couple of seconds because I could not believe the coincidence. I knew straight away God wanted to refresh me but I needed to stop gossiping. By the way, gossiping is gossiping whether you do it with your spouse or kids or just a few of your friends.

It took me a while to practise this and I have prayed that God would help me in this area. It is all part of growing up as a Christian, no one gets there in a week. Jesus calls this process of growing up, pruning. In John

15 Jesus said that He is the true vine and God is the vine dresser while we are the branches. Every branch that bears fruit, the Father will prune so it can grow and bear more fruit. Pruning can be very painful to a branch and so it is to us Christians.

Changing habits and getting rid of the old ones is not easy, that is why we need the Helper, the Holy Spirit to teach us how to grow and change.

I have been known for my short tamper ever since I was a young girl and I used to think that since I am a small person, I needed the short temper to protect myself by being very rude, which I did. That did not change as soon as I became a Christian. It took God Himself I must say, to get rid of the anger and deal with my temper. God is faithful to all of us if we ask Him to help us in areas we need help.

I struggled with unforgiveness for a very long time, hence the anger and the short temper. I could not forgive until one day a friend gave me CD's called 'Armed and dangerous' by Joyce Meyer. I listened to those CD's a million times before I could actually get it. That really helped me to learn to forgive and to do good things for people who had hurt me, even when I was still hurting.

I watch the Christian channel on Austar all the time and one day, Joel Osteen was teaching on staying cool and calm and never letting the enemy take your peace away. That I watched a dozen times. So now if I feel angry or agitated, I listen to those CD's and messages to remind me not to act out of anger. My husband made a comment one day about all this. He said 'Salome I have said this to you all the time so did it have to come from someone else for you to get the message on forgiveness?' He had taught me on forgiveness a hundred times but I just did not want to listen to him, especially if I was mad at him! Talk about being stubborn!

Here is the menu and please order help so you can start to grow up.

Here is how we can pray about this – 'Lord Jesus, please help me not to judge other people. Help me to see people the way You see them. Help me to love people unconditionally like You do. Teach me Lord how to forgive people who hurt me and show me how to pray for them as You say in your word.'

CHAPTER 9

EXPECTATIONS OF THE KINGDOM CITIZENS

I became a citizen of Australia in 2012 and there are things I never applied for, but I got them anyway just because I am now a citizen of Australia. These things come with the package, so to speak. I have to vote whether I like it or not and there is no escaping. I did not vote the first year after I became a citizen because I thought my one vote would not make a difference. What I did not know is everything in Australia is computerised, so I received a letter in the mail asking me to explain why I had not voted. I cooked up a few excuses and sent them back. I received yet another letter saying my excuses were not good enough, so I had to pay a fine. Now that got me thinking because I do not like paying fines. I paid the fine and the following year I think I was one of the first people to line up to vote. I learnt my lesson!

Now, becoming a Christian comes with expectations and excuses are not good enough for all activities in the Kingdom. Prayer is not optional in the Kingdom of God and it is an expectation from the King Himself that we commune with Him everyday. After all, this is a relationship not a religion. Jesus said in Mathew 6 v5-7, 'and when you pray, you shall not be like the hypocrites. For they love to pray standing in the synagogues and on the corners of the streets, that they may be seen by men. Assuredly,

I say to you, they have their reward. ⁶ But you, when you pray, go into your room, and when you have shut your door, pray to your Father who *is* in the secret *place;* and your Father who sees in secret will reward you openly.⁷ And when you pray, do not use vain repetitions as the heathen *do.* For they think that they will be heard for their many words."

Take note that He said when you pray (three times in the same chapter) and not if you pray which means there is an expectation that you have to pray. This is one activity we cannot negotiate on or give excuses about as Christians. The Lord expects us to pray always without ceasing. There are things in those verses that we can learn from about prayer. One, prayer is personal and confidential. Yes we can have corporate prayer too because Jesus said if we agree on anything in prayer and bring it before God, He will do it for us. Praying as a group is very biblical and throughout the bible there are stories of victories that people had after groups of people came together in prayer. God wants us to have private prayer as our main priority. We do not pray to be seen, we pray to get results from our Father, which are guaranteed in His word.

Shutting the door means this is a private activity and can be done anywhere but in a private manner, not to be applauded by other people. It is not in the length of the prayer or the eloquence of speech. God is moved by our faith and genuineness of heart. Many words are not to be our main focus but praying His will. That is why after that, Jesus taught us a model prayer commonly known as the Lord's Prayer.

In that prayer, He taught us that we must come to God as our Father and source of everything. We must have a grateful heart and always praise Him. We must approach Him not only for our personal needs but for everyone else's needs, hence the words 'Our Father.' We have to pray that His will and only His will be done on earth as it is in heaven. This is the heart of God, to see heaven on earth as we give Him 'license' through prayer to intervene on planet earth. We must acknowledge that we fail and make mistakes and ask for His forgiveness as we forgive other people too. We must ask for our daily sustenance and purpose. We must ask for protection from the enemy and pray that we do not get tempted by the enemy.

Jesus led us by example. His ministry was birthed in prayer and prayer is what He did more than the miracles. The disciples of Jesus asked Him to teach them how to pray, which means they must have seen how important this activity was in the life of Jesus. Mark 1v35, "Now in the morning, having risen a long while before daylight, He went out and departed to a solitary place; and there He prayed." Jesus would wake up well before daylight and pray in a quiet place. He did this very often because that is where He got the power to do what He did in His ministry. We cannot even think of doing life without prayer and fasting, which Jesus also taught His disciples to do. Someone said prayer and fasting are Siamese twins. You cannot do one without the other. Jesus prayed for forty days and forty nights before He started His ministry. That is a huge challenge to us, His followers. If Jesus, being God Himself, prayed and fasted for that long, what gives us the idea that we can pray for two minutes and fast half a day once a year, then expect to live victorious lives as Christians?

The expectation is that we have to fast and pray all the time. Mathew 17v21 says, "However, this kind does not go out except by prayer and fasting." The twelve disciples had asked Jesus why they had failed to cast out a demon out of a boy. They had failed as we all sometimes do, to cast out a demon and they were bold enough to ask the teacher why they had failed. Jesus did not beat about the bush, He plainly explained to them that they had no faith and that they had to fast and pray to cast out demons of that kind. That means that there are some demons that will not come out, no matter how much we scream at them!! They check our bellies first to see if we ever fast and they have a record of our prayer life. I can almost hear the demons laughing and saying, 'we are not going anywhere guys, the person trying to cast us out has never fasted or prayed.' Imagine a demon laughing at us, yet we are supposed to have dominion over them!! We need to pray and fast all the time, as well as studying the word everyday, so we know to pray the will of the Father.

Giving in the kingdom of God is one activity that the King expects us to do. Luke 6v38 says, "Give and it will be given to you: good measure, pressed down, shaken together, and running over will be put into your bosom. For with the same measure that you use, it will be measured back to you." Wow, what a promise! We often pray for a good measure, pressed down, shaken together and running over, expecting other people to pour out a blessing on us and yet sometimes we do not want to give. Giving is so rewarding and fulfilling and there is a promise attached to this activity from the King Himself. There is a lot to give to people other than just money and gifts. We can give help and support to a young girl who is struggling in her marriage. We can give advice to a friend, we can give compliments (they cost us nothing) and a word of encouragement or our time. There is really no excuse to say, "I can't give because I have got nothing to give."

People have hated the word 'give' because it has been misrepresented, sometimes even in the church. I think some of us Christians have manipulated the verse to mean that we make our pastors rich while everyone else is overlooked. Do not get me wrong, there is nothing wrong with blessing your pastor but if giving to the church leadership is highlighted every time, it can give a wrong impression altogether to the congregants. There are a lot of people in need out there who could do with a new pair of shoes (because they have never owned one). Before we give the church elder who is working full time, two pairs of shoes for her birthday, let us pause and think of a distant cousin who has never owned a pair of shoes all her life! Let us give with a purpose and the King will reward us. Again, there is nothing wrong with blessing your Church elder, it is actually biblical but I am sure the church elder would feel better if you blessed the orphan in your church too!

In every restaurant there is a dress code and some rules to follow while you are in there. Some say no casual clothes, some say smart casual but no thongs, some say after a certain time you have to dress a certain way. Most of them prohibit that you bring your own drinks (which is fair enough). Well, the Kingdom Restaurant is no different. Everything on the menu is free of course, that's already been made clear but there are some expectations as already mentioned. The King expects us to forgive people. All of them! That is one area I have had to ask for some training from the King Himself. To some people, forgiveness comes naturally but some of us need a lot of training on that. Jesus went on to say not only do we forgive our enemies, but we should pray for them and even give them food when they are hungry! Imagine that! No wonder the Lord said the road is narrow and difficult. Peter asked Jesus if seven times was the cut off number for forgiveness. I am pretty sure Peter had someone he had been hanging in there to punch or let them have it. I think he had been counting and had reached the number seven offense with the same person, so he wanted to double check with the Teacher before he told this person that he had had enough of them! Jesus then did the "Kingdom sum" that really challenges our faith. He said seventy times seven which is 490 times, the last time I checked. Wow, 490 times, who counts these things? Then I have to prepare a meal (poison free) for that person who has hurt me and then pray for them on top of that! I need tones of help in this area and I think we all do.

Maybe what we need to ask for, is lots of love and peace before we are even hurt. Maybe what we need to ask for, is a big heart that overlooks offenses before the offenses come because Jesus even promised us that offenses will come. He even said that in this world we shall have problems and tribulations, but we need to cheer up because He has overcome the world John 16v33.

'These things I have spoken to you, that in Me you may have peace. In the world you will have tribulation; but be of good cheer, I have overcome the world." I wanted Jesus to promise me that once I become a child of God, I would not have problems. I wanted the promise of a rose garden where everything is smooth running, where everybody likes me and I like them, where everything is perfect. That is my idea of church life! Well, here is a newsflash Salome. Jesus never had a smooth life with no problems, even Him being God in the flesh. He was at one stage accused of casting out demons by Beelzebub after casting out a demon. He then gave his famous talk that a kingdom divided against itself cannot stand or how could Satan cast out Satan? That silenced the opposition for a while, but did they stop looking for faults in Him? No. My friends, our purpose is to do the will of our Father in heaven but being a Christian comes with a cost and lots of expectations. Everything that is genuine in this life comes with a cost. Jesus then said, if they called Him Beelzebub, we should be ready to be called even worse but we need to cheer up, because our reward is great.

All my married friends can testify to this that everything worthwhile in this life comes with a cost. When we are dating before marriage, we do not see faults because we are madly in love. After all, we only see them at church or when we go out for dinner, all dressed up! Weddings are the best days of our lives. We take lots of photos, dressed to kill. Marriage then starts after the wedding of course. Six months later we begin to notice that the person we married has anger issues, talks a lot, is very untidy or is a shopaholic. Fights start and mood swings begin. Bring it on!! We are in it for the long-haul so we don't quit as soon as the first fight shows up on our door. I salute people who have been married longer than us because I know marriage has its ups and downs. Sometimes you want to quit and catch the next train home. I know a lot of people who wished they had not divorced their spouse and are regretting it all now. So do not give up on your marriage. I am not judging those who have divorced, but all I am saying is marriage is a lot of work. It takes a lot to stay married. It is a lifelong commitment and so is our Christian walk. Psalms 66v10-12 says,

"For You, O God, have tested us;
You have refined us as silver is refined.
[11] You brought us into the net;

You laid affliction on our backs.
¹² You have caused men to ride over our heads;
We went through fire and through water;
But You brought us out to rich fulfilment."

The Psalmist is actually thanking God for all the bad things that have happened to him. He sees his obstacles as something that has brought him into the full purposes of God. What a way to look at offense, hurts and problems! I have people in life that I secretly thank who have contributed to the person I am today. I pray before I go to work every day because of the challenges of work. When we go through trials, problems and offenses but do not see good coming out of them immediately, let us remember that God is faithful to His word. All things will definitely work together for our good; Romans 8v28.

Studying and meditating on the word of God is a must and a huge expectation in the Kingdom of God. We get our guidance and answers to the questions of our lives in the word of God. I used to think that all I had to do was recite scriptures and I would be alright, but that is not enough. Meditating is slowing down to think about what the word of God is saying and applying it in faith, in our lives.

I will never forget this, one day I was doing our devotional with my husband. We bumped into a scripture in Haggai 2, 'Consider now from this day forward, from the twenty-fourth day of the ninth month, from the day that the foundation of the LORD's temple was laid—consider it: ¹⁹ Is the seed still in the barn? As yet the vine, the fig tree, the pomegranate, and the olive tree have not yielded *fruit. But* from this day I will bless *you.*'

What a great promise from the Lord to bless us! But one thing we noticed was that the promise has a date on it. So we started thanking God for the 24th day of the ninth month of that year, 2007. We started saying "Lord thank you that from the 24th of September you will bless us." Guess what happened? On the 24th of September 2007 we got our permanent visa to stay in Australia!

> **Primary Applicant:** Salome Chifamba
> **Application Type:** Skilled - Independent (Migrant) Class BN,
> Subclass 137 - Skilled - State/Territory-nominated Independent
> **Application Date:** 19th March 2007
>
> Dear Ms Chifamba
>
> **VISA GRANTS**
>
> I am writing to advise that, on **24 September 2007**, a decision was taken to grant a Skilled - Independent (Migrant) Class BN, Subclass 137 - Skilled - State/Territory-nominated Independent visa to the following applicants:
>
> **Primary Applicant:** Salome Chifamba
> **Family members:** RUTENDO COLLETA CHIFAMBA (24/7/1999)
> RUMBIDZAI TSITSI CHIFAMBA (3/2/1995)
> KUDZAI CHIFAMBA (3/7/1991)
> FIDELIS CHIFAMBA (19/4/1965)
>
> This visa has been granted under the Skilled - Sponsored scheme which is designed to attract migrants to states and territories who need people with particular skills. In granting this visa the holder is reminded that they have entered into a mutual obligation with the sponsoring State/Territory Government. This obligation includes a commitment to live and work in the sponsoring State/Territory. The sponsoring State/Territory Government has requested that the holder contact them as soon as possible after their arrival as they may be able to assist with advice including employment related information for the holder and any working age

Not only that but my husband who had been working as a Carer for an organisation called Helping Hand, got a job as a manager and his contract stated that from the 24th of September 2007, he was starting in his new role! Look my friend, I cannot overemphasise how faithful God is! The new job that my husband got, made him move four steps up the ladder to management from being a carer, to a manager in one day!

Faith is one of the things we are expected to have in the Kingdom of God. The bible clearly says in Hebrews 11v6, "But without faith *it is* impossible to please *Him,* for he who comes to God must believe that He is and *that* He is a rewarder of those who diligently seek Him," That is very clear that God expects us to have faith so we can believe that whatever things we ask for in prayer, we will receive. Jesus told us in His word that with faith all things will be possible for us, but then He told us that the faith can start as small as a mustard seed then grow bigger. It is easy to describe faith and it is even easier to preach on it. It's living a life of faith that can be challenging. We are told to walk by faith and not by sight, but sometimes sight gets in the way of faith.

CHAPTER 10

ENTITLEMENTS OF RESTAURANT PATRONS

There are some things we are entitled to when we enter restaurants and if you do not know them, you can go in there, enjoy your meal and leave without getting what you are entitled to as a patron. There is a restaurant in Port Pirie where I live, which offers the best pancakes with cream and syrup for dessert when you order a main meal. That comes with the meal for everyone after dinner. Now if you do not know that, it is easy to pay for dessert when you can get one for free. The bible says in Hosea 4v6, "My people are destroyed for lack of knowledge. Because you have rejected knowledge, I also will reject you from being priest for Me." Lack of knowledge can make you miss out on what you are entitled to. We must study the word of God as Christians so we know what we are entitled to.

One day my car just would not start. I did not know what was wrong, it had never done that before. I must have tried very hard out of impatience to start the car and my keys broke into the ignition. Now I had two problems. One of the teachers I work with, asked me if I had any road side assistance and I said I did not. I ended up getting help from a friend who is a mechanic. I managed to start the car and went home. When I got home, I asked my husband if we had road side assistance for my car and he replied yes. We had to ring our insurance to see if we had any road side assistance and we were told we do. I asked what I was entitled to in the policy and I could not believe that for almost ten years, I had driven my car without knowing that I had road side assistance on the car. How sad is that!

As Christians, we are entitled to dominion. This was given to us right from the beginning in Genesis 1v26-28.

[26] "Then God said, "Let Us make man in Our image, according to Our likeness; let them have dominion over the fish of the sea, over the birds of the air, and over the cattle, over all the earth and over every creeping thing that creeps on the earth." [27] So God created man in His *own* image; in the image of God He created him; male and female He created them. [28] Then God blessed them, and God said to them, "Be fruitful and multiply; fill the earth and subdue it; have dominion over the fish of the sea, over the birds of the air, and over every living thing that moves on the earth."

Here are some of the definitions of dominion; control, rulership, sovereignty, government, superiority, power, leadership, rule, lordship, responsibility, right to govern or rule, influence, etc. God gave us rulership or government over the earth. We are not to sit back and watch the enemy take over the earth and run the world the way he wants to. We as children of God, are to run the show, have influence and rule over the affairs of this world (we are not given power to control other people by the way, lest we get too excited). God mentioned that we have dominion over the birds of the air, fish, animals, etc. The only animal that is not mentioned on the list is another human being.

God is waiting on us to have knowledge of what we are entitled to, so we can use what we have, to do what we are supposed to do. Lack of knowledge of this truth can make the enemy run all over our lives, when we are supposed to be the ones having control or dominion. The world is full of lost people and they are looking for a genuine government that could help them in their lives. The only government that brings genuine change in this world is the Kingdom of God. So if God gave us the Kingdom then we should pray the kingdom to come and take over the whole earth, so that the lifestyle and culture of earth matches the one in heaven. Friend, wherever you are, God wants you to reign by bringing the influence of heaven into your home, workplace and area wherever you live.

How do I do this Salome? I am glad you asked. We are all created in the image of God. God created us in His likeness and we have what He has and we can use what He used to create what we see today. God works with a tool called faith.

Hebrews 11v1-3 says, 'Now faith is the substance of things hoped for, the evidence of things not seen. [2] For by it the elders obtained a *good* testimony.[3] By faith we understand that the worlds were framed by the word of God, so that the things which are seen were not made of things which are visible.

Faith is believing that the unseen, become reality in our lives. God spoke and the things that were unseen became real on earth. He spoke and it happened and that is faith. God wants us to have that kind of faith to change the world around us. By faith, we can pray for our kids to change. By faith, we can pray that the kingdom of God invades our work places. By faith, we can pray that the kingdom of God invades all the continents and countries of the world. By faith, we can pray that the kingdom of heaven invades every sphere of life including politics, health, education, sports, social media, just to mention a few.

We as Christian should make it our goal that wherever we are, we influence the culture of that place to match that of heaven. It is our mandate from the King Himself that we take over the earth for His glory. Gone are the days that we are scared of the world, because we are a minority. Yeast is smaller than dough and you do not need much of it to make dough rise. Mathew 13 v 33, 'Another parable He spoke to them: "The kingdom of heaven is like leaven, which a woman took and hid in three measures of meal till it was all leavened." See? Yeast is smaller than dough but just one teaspoon of it will make a huge dough rise twice as much! The moral of the parable from Jesus, is that numbers in the kingdom do not count. As long we have faith to believe that the government of Heaven is behind us, we can do the work of God with no fear at all.

I like to give the example of a police officer. The officer is appointed and employed by the government to enforce law and order in society. The size of the police officer or age does not stop him from enforcing law. A huge truck driven by a six foot tall man with huge muscles, stops and pulls over when a short police officer tells him to. Why? The huge truck driver knows that the government is behind that police officer and people have to listen to him whether they like it or not. It's called authority. God gave us authority and our size or age should not be a worry to us. The government of heaven is behind us in everything we do. We can cast out demons in the name of Jesus. We can command diseases to leave peoples' bodies in the name of Jesus. We have the power and authority to do that. Luke 10v19 says, "Behold, I give you the authority to trample on serpents and scorpions, and over all the power of the enemy, and nothing shall by any means hurt you." Christian friend, how clear is that from the King Himself? Nothing shall by any means hurt us! This is where we should jump up and down with gratitude to God. So we can go ahead, with authority, pull down all the strongholds of the enemy in the name of Jesus.

We are entitled to peace. Matthew 11v28-30 says, "Come to Me, all *you* who labour and are heavy laden, and I will give you rest. [29] Take My yoke upon you and learn from Me, for I am gentle and lowly in heart, and you will find rest for your souls. [30] For My yoke *is* easy and My burden is light."

Peace is a very precious commodity in our lives. Without peace, you can go into depression easily. Without peace, you can have lack of sleep and health problems like high blood pressure. Now if something is offered for free and all I need to do is to follow the instructions, then I would grab that thing real quick. Peace is guaranteed when I come to

Jesus and take His yoke upon my shoulders. So every morning I wake up and do this swap with Jesus; I give Him my burdens and my yoke and I grab His yoke and burdens, first thing up! How comforting is that, that someone is willing to take all my burdens and my yoke for free! Friend let us give Jesus all our burdens, yes everything. Surrender it to Him.

Money does not give or buy us peace. I have seen millionaires who cannot sleep or enjoy their life (nothing against money). Fame does not give us peace, sometimes it gives us the opposite. There is nothing wrong with these things but they are not the solution to our lack of peace. There is an assurance of peace if we mix the word of God with faith. Hebrews 4v1-3 says, "Therefore, since a promise remains of entering His rest, let us fear lest any of you seem to have come short of it. [2] For indeed the gospel was preached to us as well as to them; but the word which they heard did not profit them, not being mixed with faith in those who heard *it*. [3] For we who have believed do enter that rest--- Let us rest in his word and have peace knowing that He is faithful to fulfil His word."

If I knew that my life would turn out to be like it is today, I would have slept well 20 years ago when I was worrying about some things in my life. What that tells me, is that God is in control of our lives. He has already planned our destinies and the plans that He has for us, are not to harm us but to give us a future and a hope; Jeremiah 29v11.

CONCLUSION

Go Tell A Friend

We live in a small town like I have already mentioned and buying the local paper is just a formality. We hear all the news first hand from eyewitnesses of events. News travels fast. Sometime in 2009, a new Indian restaurant opened in town and it did not take a week for the whole town to start talking about it. I don't think the owners of the restaurant had to do much advertising. The customers did it themselves.

So why don't you go and advertise this restaurant called the Kingdom of God and let everyone in your area know that there is a restaurant where meals are free, because the Son of the Owner paid for all the meals ages ago. Who would not want free food?

People might take you for a lunatic at first, but go yea therefore and tell the whole world that God is real and that He has changed your life. Remember, you do not have to explain what happens behind the scenes while the Chef prepares the meals. Your job and mine, is to hand out the menus and let everyone have a choice of what they want to have. All you have to assure them is that if it's on the menu, then the kitchen staff can handle it.

What we pray for, is that God prepares us for His work. We need to learn to spend time with our Lord every day. I do not know about you, but I love to be in the limelight. I love to draw attention to myself and be praised by friends and relatives. I like being noticed and taking credit for a lot of things in my life. It feeds my self-esteem and I feel good about myself (this is not how life should be Salome!) Recently, God has been dealing with me about this. In His word in John 15, Jesus talks about abiding in Him and Him in us. He said that is what we should do and seek Him first, then we can have fruit.

I have always wanted to spend time casting out demons and preaching, but spending time with Jesus? I would just do that quickly, looking at the clock sometimes, just to make sure I did my one hour duty! Recently the Lord has been dealing with me to spend more time in prayer, as the word says, then I can be able to bear fruit. All I wanted was to bear fruit, but I never really liked spending a lot of time praying. I am still growing in this area but wow, I think I have come a long way. I won't pick up the phone, even when my best friends call, during my prayer time. I won't even leave the room I am praying in until I am satisfied spiritually. I am no longer praying to fulfil my duty as a Christian, but I am enjoying my prayer life. I look forward to my prayer time and I am learning to listen to God more often than I used to. I guard that time jealously. I don't want to sound like I have figured it all out, but all I can say is my prayer life is growing all the time. Jesus told us to pray, then we will not even need to struggle bearing fruit. So here is what I am getting at. You and I have got work to do, but we need to be prepared for it.

Be honest and transparent with family and friends if you are weak in that area, ask for help in prayer. We cannot expect to be victorious when we are still hiding things from family. The bible says in Psalms 66v18, "If I regard iniquity in my heart, The Lord will not hear." I do not know about you, but I want God to hear me when I pray so let us pray that God creates clean hearts for us. You are guaranteed a clean heart when you ask for one.

Mark 16v15-18, has our commission from the Lord Jesus.

"Later He appeared to the eleven as they sat at the table; and He rebuked their unbelief and hardness of heart, because they did not believe those who had seen Him after He had risen. [15] And He said to them, Go into all the world and preach the gospel to every creature. ¹⁶ He who believes and is baptized will be saved; but he who does not believe will be condemned. ¹⁷ And these signs will follow those who believe: In My name they will cast out demons; they will speak with new tongues; ¹⁸ they will take up serpents; and if they drink anything deadly, it will by no means hurt them; they will lay hands on the sick, and they will recover."

The signs will follow us when we go out there and preach the good news about the Kingdom of God. I know you are thinking that you are not an ordained minister or a renowned preacher. That is fine. You do not have to be one to preach the good news. Preach the best way you can. If it is through music or books, do it. If it is through your gift of cooking, do it through that. Use your gift to reach out to the world. Philip, in the book of Acts chapter 8, was only a waiter chosen to distribute food but look at how much God used him in the city of Samaria. He was a believer, filled with the Holy Spirit and wisdom. That is enough qualification for you to be used by God.

Let us get busy dear friend, the world is waiting for the culture of heaven to take over. What are you waiting for?

Let us pray,

"Father in the name of Jesus I pray that we your citizens, like yeast go out there and influence the world. I pray that Your Spirit fills us and use us to bring the culture of heaven down here on earth Lord, for the gory of Your Name. I pray that You take over our youth Lord and invade them with Your Kingdom Lord. I pray for every marriage Lord, that You restore everything that the enemy has stolen, my Father. I pray that our little ones will grow up knowing You and filled with the Holy Spirit, even from their mother's womb. Lord I pray for every dysfunctional home, that it is healed in the name of Jesus. Lord I pray for all the drug and alcohol addicts out there, that You set them free and invade their lives with Your kingdom.

Lord I pray for every continent, every country and every nationality, that Your Kingdom takes over. Do not leave any stone unturned Lord. Invade the church Lord with Your Kingdom lifestyle and get rid of traditions that stand in the way of your word. Take over the lives of everyone reading this book, for the glory of Your name." Amen.

www.ingramcontent.com/pod-product-compliance
Lightning Source LLC
Chambersburg PA
CBHW032054150426
43194CB00006B/522